kids london

KU-051-254

a guide for 0–8s

kids london

••• ellipsis

jane lamacraft and vicky wilson

a guide for 0–8s

•••

All rights reserved. No part of this publication may be reproduced in any form without written permission from the publisher

British Library cataloguing in publication
A CIP record for this book is available from the British Library

PUBLISHED BY •••ellipsis
2 Rufus Street London N1 6PE
E MAIL ...@ellipsis.co.uk
www http://www.ellipsis.com
SERIES EDITOR Tom Neville
SERIES DESIGN Jonathan Moberly

COPYRIGHT © 2000 Ellipsis London Limited
ISBN 1 84166 029 9

PRINTING AND BINDING Hong Kong

•••ellipsis is a trademark of Ellipsis
London Limited

For a copy of the Ellipsis catalogue or
information on special quantity orders
of Ellipsis books please contact
Faye Chang
020 7739 3157 or faye@ellipsis.co.uk

kids london: a guide for 0–8s

Jane Lamacraft and Vicky Wilson 2000

contents

Introduction

Received wisdom has it that inner cities and children don't mix. But in our experience London functions as an all-weather playground, with an amazing variety of entertainment – much of it free – if you know where to look. Moreover, the capital is at last waking up to the idea that parents/carers and their children represent a significant market. Some previously very grown-up museums and galleries now organise children's activities, especially at weekends and during school holidays, and many theatres and cinemas stage children's shows. Restaurants increasingly provide crayons, colouring sheets and child-friendly service and shops are more likely to have parent-and-baby rooms, a look-and-do-touch approach, perhaps even a crèche. Our problem in compiling this guide has not been how to fill it, but which of the city's many attractions to leave out.

Kids London is aimed at the under-8s. It doesn't set out to be a comprehensive listing of all the classes, activities and facilities the capital has to offer this age-group: in general, for instance, we have left out the many excellent local parks, libraries and swimming pools that even the most cash-strapped boroughs miraculously provide (you all have your favourites and you're not going to cross London to try someone else's). We have also omitted the kinds of activity kids love but adults can only suffer – so none of those indoor adventure playgrounds where you're left sipping a cup of vending-machine coffee in a grim shed, grisly 'amusement' arcades and the like.

Instead we've concentrated on outings where there's pleasure to be had for children and adults together – activities you can enjoy alongside your children rather than places to park them while you do something else. So along with purely child-oriented attractions we have included museums and galleries, houses and gardens and famous landmarks that can be appreciated on two levels: adults can enjoy the art, architecture, landscape or history (or at worst a decent cappuccino), children the quizzes, green spaces, playgrounds or hands-on fun. We have broken many of the rules we set ourselves when we started out, but by and large we have covered only those venues that provide something special for families. All the houses and gardens listed, for instance, have extensive grounds that function as parks, often with additional attractions such as mazes or model railways; parks have been included only when they offer something different from the best local venues, whether through their size, spectacular landscaping or the range of activities on offer; all the museums we've chosen have aspects of their collections that appeal to under-8s without any help from trails or art trolleys, so you can visit at any time; and for the hands-on section we've included only drop-in activities, most of which are fun for adults and children together. The restaurants we have selected all offer something beyond the crayons and kids' menus that are becoming almost standard service (among the chains, both TGI Friday and PizzaExpress deserve special commendation in this respect). The availability of food can be crucial to the success of the outing, so mentions of nearby child-friendly eateries are included within many entries.

Inevitably the selection in this guide to some extent reflects our own interests and prejudices, but we can assure you that we and our children – and our children's friends/friends' children – have visited and enjoyed everything you'll find on the following pages (with the exception of the London Eye, unfinished as we went to press). We have tried to give you the benefit of the knowledge we wished we'd had on our first trips – because there's nothing more annoying than finding out too late that had you turned left instead of right you would have discovered the big adventure playground rather than the two-swings-and-a-seesaw affair that left your children bored and complaining, that the museum café where you've promised them lunch doesn't exist, or that the best pictures were in that last room you were too stressed to bother with. Our research often felt exhausting as well as exhaustive – and we don't suggest you attempt everything listed in each entry at one go. With small children, less can often be more fun. Rather, our aim (and the reason for the full descriptions instead of just listings) is to help you to get the most out of your visits by making sure you are aware of the best each venue has to offer.

On a practical note: we have of course striven to give you the most up-to-date information, but opening times, prices and so on do change. (Where no admission charges are listed, entry is free.) Museums and landmarks occasionally close for maintenance or special events and many attractions – the Science Museum, the Horniman, the British Museum, Coram's Fields and Crystal Palace Park to name just a few – are undergoing substantial millennial improvements which in the short term will lead to disruption and sometimes the temporary closure of galleries or features. So do telephone to check before setting out. So too for disabled access, which we have mentioned only when venues are not accessible (though many places claimed to be in the process of improving wheelchair access). Most major museums and galleries now have websites providing updated information for visitors, and we have listed website addresses where available. We have listed the closest Underground station; there may be others almost as close on other lines, particularly in central London.

We hope *Kids London* will inspire you to try not only the things we've enjoyed but also some of the seasonal events we've shunned for lack of space. London is a big, busy, culturally diverse and fascinating city in which there is always something going on to fuel children's imaginations:

the Lord Mayor's show in November; the dazzling display of lights, shop windows and store Santas at Christmas time; the London Marathon; the calendar of festivals and community celebrations, from Chinese New Year to the Notting Hill Carnival. Even those parts of London adults regularly trudge through only grudgingly – such as its railway stations or Heathrow Airport – can provide entertainment for children.

You will, of course, have your own favourites. We'd like to hear about them for future editions. Let us know, either by post or by email to kids@ellipsis.co.uk.

ACKNOWLEDGEMENTS
Our thanks to publisher Tom Neville for giving us the chance to write this book in the first place; to photographers Keith Collie and Emerald Fitzgerald for all their hard work; and to the staff at the many galleries, museums and other venues who provided help. Thanks too for their suggestions and help with research to: Dermot Wilson, Janet, Sam and Katie South, Max Davey, Alice Mills, Sophie Neville, Rachel Poynor, Nick Deschamps and the staff and children of Bemerton UFEC. Most of all to Nancy Wilson and Henry Esterson for their energetic and enthusiastic consumer-testing.

outdoor spaces

Battersea Park

Designed and built in the 1850s, Battersea Park is one of London's most varied green spaces, one that appeals to an interesting cross section of users. Its gently sloping lawns are popular with the picnickers of Pimlico and Chelsea on sunny Sundays, while in its beautiful walled gardens gentlemen of a certain age doze as they listen to the cricket on their personal stereos; sporty types come here for the tennis courts, bowling green and all-weather pitches, while rollerbladers and cyclists career along the carriage drives (see page 7.12). Those looking for a quieter time can stroll through the winding walkways of the sub-tropical gardens and around the lake, admiring plants, sculptures (by Henry Moore and Barbara Hepworth among others), cascades and water fowl. On the other side of the park the riverside walk extends from Albert Bridge to Chelsea Bridge via the Peace Pagoda, a gift from a Japanese Buddhist order.

If you're not a regular your first port of call should probably be the Park Office near Albert Bridge Road (020 8871 7530), or the Pump House (020 8871 7572) in the south-east corner of the park, where you can collect a map and a leaflet giving details of everything on offer. You can also pick up a nature trail, which will take you butterfly-, frog- and squirrel-spotting in the Wilderness and the Meadow.

The most popular destination for families is the Children's Zoo (open Easter to October daily, 10.00–17.00; winter weekends, 11.00–15.00; telephone 020 8871 7540): inhabitants include cows, snakes, monkeys and – most entertainingly – otters and meerkats. There are roundabouts, pony rides (rather extortionate), and a shop which unfortunately, since it is also the way-out, is unavoidable. Various activities – such as treasure hunts, face painting, keeper talks, and animal 'art attacks' – are organised at the zoo during the spring and summer months. Admission to the zoo is £1.45 for adults and 70p for children (under-2s free).

outdoor spaces

Battersea Park

More animals can be found in the deer enclosure, alongside which towards the south-east of the park is the boating lake (open in summer) and a lakeside café.

For 5- to 16-year-olds there is a terrific adventure playground in the south-west corner providing both indoor and outdoor activities. As well as a very large climbing frame of brightly coloured bridges, ropes and high- and low-level walkways, there is table tennis, pool and computer games. The playground is free and fully staffed; activities tend to be weather-dependent and organised on a first-come, first-served basis. (Open termtime Tuesday to Friday, 15.30–19.00; Saturday and Sunday, 11.00–18.00; during school holidays daily, 11.00–18.00; telephone 020 8871 7539.) Next door there's a lovely playground for younger children, with swings, slide, wooden train and picnic tables, and a one o'clock centre for under-5s (open Monday to Friday, 13.00–16.00; telephone 020 8871 7541).

Annual attractions include the Harness Horse Parade at Easter, the summer Teddy Bears' Picnic and November fireworks.

A major restoration programme is under way; as a result some areas of the park are likely to be zoned off over the next few years. JL

ADDRESS Albert Bridge Road, London SW11 (entry to park also from Queens Circus or Queenstown Road; pedestrian access from Prince of Wales Drive) (park office 020 8871 7530)
OPEN daily, from 7.00
GETTING THERE Battersea Park or Queenstown Road rail; Sloane Square Underground; car parks by Chelsea Bridge Gate, Rosary Gate, Albert Bridge Gate and the athletics track

Camley Street Natural Park

Pause outside to admire the skeletons of the five former gas-holders used as a backdrop in television commercials, pop videos and filmed gritty urban realism, then enter Camley Street Natural Park, one of more than 50 inner-city nature reserves run by the London Wildlife Trust.

Once inside, it's charming. The circular route leads you past beds planted with herbs, a wildflower meadow, a marsh, a pond and areas of woodland arranged as a series of 'secret gardens', each new space a revelation (the whole circuit includes several steps, but a shorter route is buggy friendly). Some new features are labelled and explained – for instance the pond, designed with a shallow end so young frogs can crawl out and crevices in which to grow the plants that provide food and shelter for the insects the frogs feed on. There's an impressive variety of birds, and even I could recognise bluebells, flag irises, celandines and lots of that white stuff we used to call 'bad man's baccy'. The path itself is a delight for small children, with logs and railway sleepers along the way to sit or climb on, a noisy wooden bridge, wooden steps and a tunnel of hawthorn and buddleia. You can try your hand at pond-dipping with the nets provided any time, and during the summer holidays the staff organise a variety of nature trails and arts and crafts activities.

The park is not a play space, but there is a green area with a central sculpture for sitting on to the left of the visitors' centre where children too can run wild. vw

ADDRESS 12 Camley Street, London NW1 (020 7833 2311)
OPEN Monday to Thursday, 9.00–17.00; Saturday and Sunday, 11.00–17.00 summer; 10.00–16.00 winter
GETTING THERE King's Cross Underground
BUGGIES/WHEELCHAIR ACCESS restricted route only

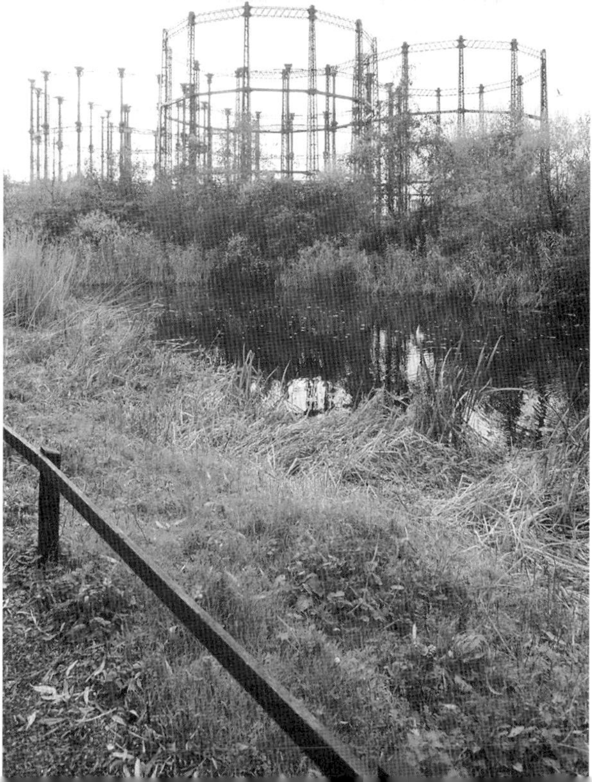

Coram's Fields

Londoners have Thomas Coram (c. 1688–1751) to thank for this wonderful family-oriented park and playground. A retired sea captain living in Rotherhithe, he was so moved by the plight of London's abandoned and destitute children that in 1741 he founded a hospital 'for the Maintenance and Education of Exposed and Deserted Children'.

His foundling hospital opened initially in temporary accommodation in Hatton Garden: children who were left in its care were given new names (the first two were called Thomas and Eunice, after Coram and his wife) and their mothers encouraged to leave identifying 'tokens' – beads, brooches, even beer labels – in case they should ever be in a position to reclaim their child. A few years later the hospital moved to new premises here in Bloomsbury, where it remained until it was relocated outside London in the 1920s. The hospital buildings were demolished in 1926 – the colonnades which had marked the boundary of its gardens are more or less all that remains – but a public campaign succeeded in keeping the site as a children's playground. Coram's Fields officially opened in 1936.

At the time of writing Coram's Fields was undergoing a major facelift, due to be completed by Easter 2000 and promising among other things improved play areas, paddling pool and landscaping. But even without the upgrade, this is a lovely, protected place for children. For a start, there are no dogs, no glass bottles, no alcohol, and no adults unless accompanied by a child. Good behaviour is actively encouraged: the noticeboard near the entrance tells you where to complain if any children are being particularly obnoxious.

Along the east side are climbing frames, sandpits and other play areas aimed at the under-5s and children with disabilities. A small café selling snacks of the ice cream/soup/sandwich variety is close by, which means you can grab a coffee while your children play. Some good play equipment

for older children is towards the rear of the park, near the sports pitches – we particularly recommend the swinging tyre and the mushroom pulley.

Under the west colonnades is a small city farm with sheep, goats, guinea pigs, rabbits and so on. Peacocks, chickens and ducks stroll free (so you do have to watch your step, dogs or no dogs). The park's central area, which is grassy and shaded by tall trees, is popular for picnics. A new paddling pool is planned, with the old one being turned into fountains.

There's an under-5s drop-in which meets during termtime in the Colonnades, and summer sports classes organised during school holidays. The (rather spartan) guide hall can be hired for children's parties. JL

ADDRESS 93 Guilford Street, London WC1 (020 7837 6138 during office hours)
OPEN daily, 9.30–20.00 summer; 9.30–17.00 winter, depending on daylight hours
GETTING THERE Russell Square Underground

Crystal Palace Park

It is more than 63 years since the great Crystal Palace burned down, but there's still plenty here to lure people Penge-ward – though a major improvements programme currently under way means that the park won't be at its best until at least 2001 (temporary closures during redevelopment make it advisable to telephone before setting out to check what's available). On arrival, your first stop should be the information kiosk (near the main Penge entrance in Thicket Road) to get a map showing all the attractions and giving details of any special activities.

The park's party piece is its herd of dinosaur-like monsters which have been standing moodily by the boating lake since the 1850s. They may be anatomically inaccurate (they were made before anyone knew much about dinosaurs) but they are still pretty impressive when you wend your way across bridges and walkways to catch your first glimpse of them. At the time of writing, the dinosaurs were being restored. The boating lake was also closed for repairs, so unfortunately the pedalo boats – wonderful fun on fine days – are out of action for summer 2000 at the least.

The maze, meanwhile, is a grand place to let children go rushing about whooping and yelling while you sit and relax on the grass (though beware gaps in the maze through which small children might be tempted to escape into the park beyond). At this point you might want to hop on the Paxton Flier land train (more of a trundler, actually) and head for the mini funfair, which is open daily April to September and on weekends, weather permitting, from October to March. It has some quaint rides suitable for smaller children, as well as a bouncy castle and crazy golf.

There is a swing-park and a drop-in one o'clock club for under-5s (which despite its name is open weekdays from 9.30 to 12.30, 13.00 to 16.00). It costs £2.40 per child. There are charges for many of the other activities too, and by the end of the day you can find you've spent quite

a tidy sum. There are cafés and refreshment kiosks dotted about, but they are basic and fairly charmless – better to take your own food if you're making a day of it and eat at one of the numerous picnic tables. Oh, and the toilets are less than salubrious. But let's not nitpick. This is a great family park – and should be even better once all the repairs and improvements have been carried out. Other likely changes include the restoration of original landscaping according to the plans of Crystal Palace's designer Joseph Paxton (1801–65), improvements to the woodland garden and a pet farm to replace the old farmyard zoo. JL

ADDRESS Thicket Road, London SE20
(020 8778 9612)
OPEN daily, from 7.30 until half an hour
before dusk
GETTING THERE Crystal Palace rail;
parking on side streets nearby
BUGGIES/WHEELCHAIR ACCESS plenty of
suitable paths

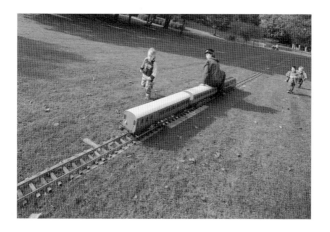

Golders Hill Park and Hampstead Heath

Golders Hill Park, off North End Road, is the tamest corner of Hampstead Heath's 320 hectares of swimming ponds and bird sanctuaries, woodland and grassy hills where you could almost forget you're in London if it weren't for the crowds and the spectacular views of the city.

Just beside the entrance is the refreshment pavilion which serves pasta and swish sandwiches and has a stall that offers 14 flavours of what I rate as the most delicious Italian ice cream this side of Rome. Walk to the animal enclosures via the formally planted walled garden with its exotic plants, animal topiary and bizarre fountain with a cherub holding a fish aloft and down the track through the trees where bridges criss-cross a man-made stream. The animals are good value, with wallabies, blackbuck antelopes with corkscrew horns and a variety of unusual birds as well as the ever-popular flamingos. Beyond the enclosures are a single large climbing frame and a pathetically small dog-free zone with a sandpit. The nicest place to relax is the more natural, tree-planted area to the right of the enclosures and this is also a good place to play.

As long as you don't have a buggy to cope with, it's worth taking the path through the hilly, wooded West Heath – a delightful play area but also a notorious gay men's cruising ground, so watch out for spent condoms in the part furthest from the road – to The Hill and the recently restored Pergola. The Hill is a beautifully planted dog-free garden with a hill that's ideal for rolling down and a pond where we've seen tadpoles and newts. The Pergola is an enormous double-height snaking structure with views over the Heath, planted with wisteria and clematis as well as kiwi fruit and Chile potato vines. Both were designed in 1905–06 by Thomas Mawson for Lord Leverhulme – owner of The Hill (later Inverforth House) and creator of the model industrial town of Port Sunlight near Liverpool – as part of an ambitious landscaping programme that

Golders Hill Park and Hampstead Heath

involved raising the gardens by some 10 metres using spoil from the tunnelling involved in extending the Northern Line.

Anyone who regularly visits the Heath has their favourite walks and spots. Ours include a picnic on the grassy slope overlooking the Model Boating Pond by Millfield Lane followed by a walk past the bird sanctuary (the first pond on the right) and up the hill (bearing right) through grassland and woods to Kenwood House – a seventeenth-century country seat acquired by George III's chief justice William Murray, 1st Earl of Mansfield, in 1754 and thoroughly messed up by Robert Adam in the 1760s – where you can take tea in the garden of the Brew House. Adults shouldn't miss the Rembrandt self-portrait (c. 1665) and Vermeer's 'The Guitar Player' (c. 1672) in the Dining Room; children enjoy the contemporary Dutch paintings of ships in this room, the many pictures of children – in particular the Reynolds paintings in the Upper Hall and Joseph Wright of Derby's dramatically lit 'Two Girls Dressing a Kitten' (the mischievous expressions of the girls and dismay of the kitten are all too familiar) in Lord Mansfield's Dressing Room – and the frieze of lions and pink, blue and gold Barbieland splendour of the Library.

On other days we take the path between the two most northerly ponds off East Heath Road up through the woods to the top of the hill, which is another good picnic spot. You can fly kites here, but enthusiasts prefer the more crowded Parliament Hill to the east with its stunning views as far as the Crystal Palace telecommunications mast, with the Post Office Tower, St Paul's, the Millennium Dome, Canary Wharf and Battersea Power Station in between.

On the Gospel Oak side of Parliament Hill are the Parliament Hill lido open-air pool and two playgrounds, one a traditional affair with a large paddling pool, the other, next to the one o'clock club, an adventure play-

park for 5–12s (sometimes closed to the public when used by school groups in termtime) in which climbing equipment is surrounded by a circular walkway of interconnected planks at different levels ideal for under-8s. The proximity to the North London Line makes this a good bet for trainspotters. The Parliament Hill café – depressing inside but with plenty of outdoor seating – serves excellent pasta along with the usual jacket potatoes, sandwiches and cakes. If it rains, the Information Centre has exhibitions about the Heath's wildlife and history.

The Corporation of London organises inflatable playstructures, children's entertainers and brass-, steel- and jazz-band concerts in Golders Hill Park and Parliament Hill at weekends and holiday periods throughout the summer, and in July and August there are pop-classical concerts at Kenwood Lakeside on Saturday evenings. But for me the Heath is best enjoyed as entertainment in its own right – go forth and explore. VW

ADDRESS North End Road, London NW11/Millfield Lane, London N6/ East Heath Road, London NW3/Gordon House Road, London NW5
OPEN Information Centre: March to October, Wednesday to Friday, 13.00–17.00; Saturday and Sunday, 10.00–12.30 and 13.00–16.00; November to February, closes at 16.00; Kenwood House: daily, April to September, 10.00–18.00; October to March, 10.00–16.00; Golders Hill café: closed in December and January; Parliament Hill café: closed on Mondays from October to February
GETTING THERE Golders Green Underground; Hampstead Heath, Gospel Oak rail; car parks at Jack Straw's Castle, North End Road/East Heath Road/Gospel Oak; free parking on North End Road and Millfield Lane
BUGGIES/WHEELCHAIR ACCESS Kenwood House: ground floor only

Greenwich Park

Greenwich Park is the oldest enclosed royal park in London. At one time in effect the gardens of Greenwich Palace, a favourite royal residence of Henrys VII and VIII, today it's one of London's most attractive parks.

Perhaps it's because it's perched high above the Thames, looking down over the city, that it seems so pleasantly apart from the urban sprawl. At its highest point it is almost 52 metres above sea level, and the views – of Wren's Naval College, the Queen's House, Canary Wharf, the Millennium Dome, as far as St Paul's and Tower Bridge – are tremendous.

The large, open slopes are great for children to run up and down and for generally letting off steam (though not ideal for pushing buggies). Other highlights for children include, in the lower, north-east corner, the large, well-equipped playground where free children's entertainments are held during the school summer holidays. Next door is the children's boating lake (open during the summer) which is reassuringly shallow.

Also interesting for children is the deer park – so gather your strength, stride up the steepish hill to the Blackheath side (the starting point of the annual London Marathon), and head for the Wilderness where red and fallow deer can be glimpsed grazing. The adjoining flower garden is very pretty and gratifyingly free of dogs, bikes, radios and ball games; it boasts a small lake and some rather well-fed ducks and squirrels. In the summer there are Sunday concerts at the nearby bandstand.

You can take a break at the café on Blackheath Avenue (outdoor seating for fine weather) before heading for the park's most famous landmark, the Royal Observatory. Home of Greenwich Mean Time, it is slap-bang on the Prime Meridian – the imaginary north–south line from which every place on earth defines its longitude. Stand astride the Prime Meridian Line – most visitors do – and you're in both eastern and western hemispheres. Once the home of the first astronomer royal John Flamsteed (1646–

1719), the Observatory has much inside for visitors to see, including John ('Longitude') Harrison's timepieces, a *camera obscura*, an interactive computer 'Astroweb', and Britain's largest refracting telescope. However, this really isn't a place for the under-8s, and is decidedly buggy-unfriendly.

Greenwich Park rubs shoulders with a number of other attractions, the biggest and best being the National Maritime Museum (see page 3.16). Blackheath itself is good for kite flying. The Fan Museum, at 12 Crooms Hill (020 8305 1441), is tiny and devoted entirely to, yes, fans. Some children might like it, but my son isn't one of them. However, the museum does have a rather wonderful, lavishly decorated Orangery where, for £4.50, you can take afternoon tea (Tuesdays and Sundays) while your children enjoy spotting all the painted butterflies, spiders, ladybirds and bees hidden in the decor.

Towards Greenwich Pier is the arty-crafty Greenwich Market (liveliest on Saturdays and Sundays) and the Cutty Sark, the fastest tea clipper ever built and itself worth a visit (open Monday to Saturday, 10.00–18.00, Sunday, 12.00–18.00; 020 8858 3445). JL

ADDRESS entrances to Greenwich Park on Charlton Way, London SE3, Crooms Hill, SE10, Maze Hill, SE3/SE10 and behind the National Maritime Museum (020 8858 2608) on Romney Road, SE10
OPEN daily, dawn to dusk
GETTING THERE Maze Hill or Greenwich rail; by bus from North Greenwich Underground; DLR to Cutty Sark. River boat services operate from Westminster (Westminster Passenger Services, 020 7930 4097) and from Embankment and the Tower of London (Catamaran Cruisers, 020 7987 1185)
BUGGIES/WHEELCHAIR ACCESS only if you don't mind hills

Highgate Wood

This swathe of 28 hectares of woodland provides an idyllic playground. It is thought the area has been wooded since the last ice age, and the history trail, which you can follow by picking up a leaflet from the information centre beside the café, takes you past ancient pottery kilns dating from AD 50–150, iron-age earthworks and examples of the wood's management practice over the past 200 years. Or simply walk around and enjoy the beauty of the oak, hornbeam, beech and holly trees and the birdsong, which makes it hard to believe you're so near central London.

In the south-west corner is a large, organic-looking playground arranged on several levels with plenty of places to sit. There's a separate under-5s enclosure, though much of the equipment in the main area is also suitable for younger children. Check out the wobbly bridge and the three interconnected pavilions with musical instruments and a periscope on their inner panels.

The Oshobasho café in the centre of the woods has copious outdoor seating in a courtyard surrounded by flowering shrubs and trees. Popular with laptop-equipped workers and couples enjoying a pre-prandial glass of wine as well as families, it serves excellent salads and sandwiches, a choice of three or four hot vegetarian dishes, good coffee and indifferent cakes. Children's portions are available, but the limited selection means this is not a place to bring fussy eaters – nor little monsters, to judge by the several notices asking you to keep your children under control. VW

ADDRESS Muswell Hill Road, London NW10 (020 8444 6129)
OPEN café: Tuesday to Sunday, 8.30 to half an hour before dusk
GETTING THERE Highgate Underground; free parking on side streets

outdoor spaces

Paddington Street Playground

Paddington Street playground is but a postage stamp compared with the other parks and play areas included in this guide. Not only is it tiny, it offers no spectacular climbing frames, paddling pools or mini-zoos. But what makes this well-kept little playground special is its location: a stone's throw from Marylebone High Street (home to the fashionable likes of the Conran Shop and Aveda) and only a short walk from Oxford Street. As such it is a children's oasis in the midst of West End retail frenzy and well worth knowing about when, having exhausted your credit card, you need to tire your kids out too. It's also very handy for the Wallace Collection (see page 4.76).

The playground is part of Paddington Street Gardens, which occupy the site of a former burial ground (one rather grand mausoleum remains) and which during sunny lunch-hours are packed with sandwich-eating office workers.

Tucked in one corner of the gardens, pleasantly shaded by trees, the playground features a pair of climbing frames, a slide, swings and ride-on equipment ideal for toddlers to 8-year-olds. It also has picnic tables, and benches on which parents can often be seen at weekends drinking coffee bought from Starbucks on Marylebone High Street (for hungry kids, there are cafés in Moxon Street selling take-away chips). What's more, the park's public toilets – several-times winner of the Westminster Loo of the Year award (really) – are immaculately clean, boasting illustrated tiles and even piped music. JL

ADDRESS Paddington Street, London W1
OPEN usually 8.15 until half an hour before the park is locked at dusk
GETTING THERE Baker Street Underground

Regent's Park

As with Richmond Park (see page 1.36), the history of Regent's Park is a murky tale of royal appropriation and exploitation of land at the expense of the public, with a fairytale ending in which the area is restored to its rightful owners. Go forth and enjoy what's yours!

Regent's Park originally formed part of the vast royal hunting grounds appropriated by Henry VIII (1491–1547). In 1646 Charles I mortgaged it to two of his supporters to pay for arms during the Civil War; during Oliver Cromwell's interregnum the land was sold and stripped of trees to pay debts. In 1760 George III agreed to receive income from the Civil List in return for surrendering rents from the Crown Estate to parliament; in 1811, as the area south of Marylebone Road was becoming fashionable, the Crown decided not to renew tenants' leases and John Nash was commissioned to design a vast round park surrounded by palatial terraces and containing a lake and canal, 56 villas 'for the wealthy and the good' and a retreat for the Prince Regent. In the end only eight villas were built and access was restricted to people living in surrounding property, those with carriages, and societies including the new Zoological Society, the Royal Botanic Society and Toxophilite, which introduced archery and flooded its land in winter for the London Skating Club. By the mid 1830s, however, mounting concern about the need to provide open-air recreation for the poor as well as the rich led to the partial opening of the park to the public.

The most interesting area today is the south side. At the extreme south-east corner (entered from St Andrew's Gate) is the English Garden, a haven of grassy hills with what it is to be hoped is a permanent exhibition of 19 granite sculptures by artist Ronald Rae – a rare successful integration of art and landscape. Children can touch the giant blocks of stone, lean on them, climb them, and from Rae's hands the granite looks as soft

and inviting as sandstone. Particularly popular with our party were the life-size 'Wounded Elephant' (1990) and 'Horse' (1994), both near the gate. Immediately to the west are the formal Italianate Avenue Gardens, laid out by William Andrew Nesfield (designer of the terraces in front of the Palm House at Kew, see page 5.22) in 1863 (his son, Markham, landscaped the English Garden, an illustration of how rapidly tastes change). The rigid symmetry, bright flowers and three-tiered fountains make this my daughter's favourite part of the park. Immediately to the west is the Marylebone Green children's playground, which has two large pieces of climbing equipment, see-saws, swings, three roundabouts, a huge sandpit with little houses in it, and picnic tables.

The best café is at the far side of Queen Mary's Gardens (west again), though there are also mobile refreshment kiosks near the playgrounds and smaller cafés just north of Chester Road at the north end of the Avenue Gardens and beside the tennis courts, where you can watch the games for entertainment. Queen Mary's Gardens, created in the early 1930s, are well worth a visit. The rose garden – surrounded by pillars draped with swags of climbers and accommodating some 30,000 plants of 400 different varieties – is one of London's finest: enjoy the scent, colour and ludicrous names. The landscaped mound behind the lake and the maze of paths and nooks separated by low hedges beside the Triton fountain are good for playing in (and lovers' trysts). The gardens also contain lawns with striped deckchairs for nannies less adventurous than Mary Poppins, and the Open Air Theatre, where you can see Shakespeare, a musical and a children's play from the end of May to early September. The pavilion-style café has plenty of outdoor seating among the roses and serves a limited range of hot food plus salads, sandwiches, good cakes, a children's menu (£2.50 school age, £1.50 toddlers) and ice cream. There's also a

small playground, though unfortunately it's not overlooked by any of the seating.

Further west is a large boating lake with six wooded islands, one of the city's most impressive collections of wildfowl, including a pair of black swans, plenty of weeping willows and fine views of The Holme, designed by Decimus Burton (see Kew, page 5.22), the son of one of Nash's builders, in 1818 when he was only 18. There's also a shallow children's lake with pedalos that weave around the central island like errant yellow ducklings. The nearby Hanover Gate playground is our favourite – pleasantly shady, with views of the shining golden dome of the London Central Mosque.

The area north of the lake is basically a large green space for sports and picnicking. The Gloucester Gate playground is disappointingly much the same as the other two, though the area immediately to the south has lots of small mounds that are fun to play on. The nearest café (sandwiches, cakes and lots of outdoor seating) is further south, down the tree-lined Broad Walk, past the fountain donated to the British nation by Mr Cowasjee Jehangir Ready-Money in 1869 in recognition of the protection afforded him and his Parsee countrymen under British rule in India.

There is usually children's entertainment during the holidays at one of the playgrounds – telephone for details – and the park hosts special events including the Music Village Festival, Tango al Fresco and the Strollerthon. VW

ADDRESS Regent's Park, London NW1 (020 7486 7905)
OPEN daily, 7.00 to dusk
GETTING THERE Regent's Park Underground

Richmond Park

Richmond Park, which extends over 1000 hectares, was enclosed in 1637 by Charles I as a hunting park in the face of considerable opposition following the compulsory purchase of farms and estates. Today it is home to some 300 red deer and 400 dappled deer and is an area for nature conservation rather than destruction.

Unlike Hampstead Heath (see page 1.16), Richmond Park rarely feels crowded – picnickers tend to congregate around the ponds and car parks and it's easy to escape the throng – while its sheer size and glorious expanses of grass, bracken and mature trees make it the most convincing ersatz-countryside experience London has to offer. You shouldn't approach the deer, which move around in groups of 30 or so, between May and July, when the stags are rutting, or in October and November when the does are protective of their young, but at other times of year they'll approach you and display an unseemly curiosity in what you're eating. The park is criss-crossed by separate paths for cars, cycles and horses and ringed by four riding stables, all of which do half-hour pony rides for over-2s, bookable in advance.

The Richmond landscape is much flatter and less differentiated than Hampstead, and almost anywhere you choose to stop makes a wonderful natural playground for children (especially if there's a fallen tree nearby). However, it's also worth exploring the Isabella Plantation, a dog-free enclosed garden of around 16 hectares towards the park's southern tip, which I rate along with Syon Park (see page 5.30) as London's most beautiful garden. The plantation was enclosed in 1831, when most of the trees were established, though the garden itself was laid out by park superintendent George Thompson in 1953. The huge, densely planted trees and shrubs, especially the azaleas and the giant rhododendrons with wonderfully shaped branches which dominate, are interrupted by glades that

make perfect places to sit, hide or play. Walk along by the stream, crossing from side to side via the wooden bridges, then head through the small wood to Thomson's Pond, which is surrounded by Japanese irises and has ducks, frogs, huge carp, waterlilies and a fun bridge made from upended logs arranged like stepping stones. The sloping lawn on the far side is our favourite place to relax; older children let loose to explore will find their own play places.

You can't picnic in Isabella Plantation, though a picnic is very much part of the Richmond Park experience. Many of the car parks have refreshment kiosks selling hot dogs, cakes, ice creams and drinks; otherwise the slightly tatty Pembroke Lodge has a café serving sandwiches, cakes, cream teas and two hot dishes. The limited choice of food is more than compensated for by the outside terrace with its stunning view west, below which is a steeply sloping hillside that's a delight for over-5s. The extensive dog-free grounds have squirrels that eat from your hand.

Don't bother with the playground (a couple of roundabouts, large sandpit, swings, small slide) that can be reached through a gate in the grounds just before you come to Henry VIII's mound, from which you can see St Paul's Cathedral 10 miles away – the hill leading to it with its spreading conifers, tree trunks and vast expanse of grass is much more fun. VW

ADDRESS FOR INFORMATION Holly Lodge, Richmond Park, Surrey TW10 (020 8948 3209)
GETTING THERE Richmond Underground; BUS 72, 74, 85, 371; several free car parks
BUGGIES/WHEELCHAIR ACCESS on cycle lanes only

South Bank

The South Bank is much maligned – and even its staunchest fans admit that the signposting and circulation are baffling and some of the spaces dank and depressing. But in its present underdeveloped state it offers riverside walks and culture, free entertainment and architecture – a day of unashamedly urban pleasures.

Apart from the Hayward Gallery, whose exhibitions always include some provision for children, the only attractions that require serious money are the London Aquarium (see page 2.6) and the London Eye (see page 6.2). Otherwise, you can spend a whole day sampling free entertainment along the broad, paved walkway that runs alongside the Thames, where children can play in safety, enjoy the sea-monster/dolphin lamp-posts, watch the boats or climb on the many sculptures – the arena surrounded by walls in the shape of fragments of a Moebius strip in front of the National Theatre and the three polished chrome domes, the largest fronted by wavy antennae, beside the Queen Elizabeth Hall are favourites. The ramp under Hungerford Bridge when a train thunders overhead (cf. *Cabaret*) never fails to delight.

The journey from west to east could be a chronological exhibition of post-war British values as expressed through architecture. The Royal Festival Hall (1951), once the flagship of a newly created Welfare State and now home to the New-Labour-styled Peoples Palace restaurant, displays a well-funded elegance (for a glimpse of the high standards envisaged for the common woman in the 1950s, check out the opulent detailing in the toilets). The dramatic brutalism of the National Theatre speaks of a late-60s rebellion that didn't quite have the courage of its convictions (note how the concrete is patterned with woodgrain). The funky aesthetic of Gabriel's Wharf – due to be redeveloped as housing in 2001 – reflects the self-help ethic of Coin Street Community Builders, which since 1984

has developed the adjacent site as co-op housing. Oxo Wharf, CSCB's permanent development begun in 1996, is sterile by comparison.

As for the attractions, Jubilee Gardens, dwarfed by the skeletal big wheel, has a playground with a range of climbing equipment. The Royal Festival Hall hosts free exhibitions in the foyer and free concerts (usually jazz or world music) from Wednesday to Sunday, 12.30–14.00. The self-service Aroma café has tables overlooking the exhibition and performance spaces (the ramp between the café and gallery is a crowd-puller for toddlers). Sometimes there are concerts and dancing outside and even on a quiet day you'll find a couple of street performers.

The trendy Film Café – lilac columns, aluminium tables and a picture of Mary Poppins outside – serves good food and rip-off children's lunchboxes (£2.20 for fruit, Hula Hoops, a chocolate biscuit and a drink), though you do get entertainment via the numerous video monitors. Or continue east to Gabriel's Wharf, where you can eat at the Gourmet Pizza Company, Studio Six or House of Crêpes and browse in the crafts shops. A big draw for children here are Friedel Buecking's sculptures – some 20 knee-high rocking pigs, cats, horses and sheep that youngsters can swarm on. The Museum of Me at Oxo Wharf has a changing series of free exhibitions.

Inevitably, the South Bank will be developed and its present feeling of an old-fashioned seafront promenade with a gallery or two thrown in will be lost to commercialism as shops, cafés and amusement arcades fill the spaces at present deemed 'wasted'. Enjoy it while you can. VW

ADDRESS The Queen's Walk, London SE1 (020 7960 4242)
WEBSITE www.sbc.org.uk
GETTING THERE Waterloo Underground

Victoria Park

Established in 1845 following a petition to the Queen signed by 30,000 local residents in response to a report identifying the area's high mortality rate which claimed a park would 'probably diminish the annual deaths by several thousands ... and add several years to the lives of the entire population', Victoria Park is still well used by East Enders – the playground attendant told me it attracts up to 1000 visitors on a hot summer's day, and you can't see the grass for picnics. It's also – along with Golders Hill Park (see page 1.16) – a favourite outing destination for my daughter's north London nursery, perhaps because the vast open spaces provide plentiful opportunities for letting off steam while the large playground can easily accommodate a group of 30.

The park is bisected by Grove Road. If you're visiting with small children by car or from Bethnal Green Underground, the smaller west side is all you'll need (I'd never set foot in the east side until I came to research this book). The west side has a good playground adjacent to Grove Road with a helter skelter and a climbing frame in the shape of a train in addition to the usual equipment. There's a toddlers' area to the north and a more challenging climbing frame to the south which is fenced off. Beware the accident-inducing roundabout – and bear in mind that the size of the playground can make it difficult to supervise two young children with separate agendas.

The park is distinguished by attractive dark-blue-painted wrought-iron work used for fencing, gates, lamp-posts lining the paved internal cycling roads and ornamental bridges over the Grand Union and Hertford Union canals.

A circular pavilion directly south of the playground houses a café that serves food of the chicken nuggets/jacket potatoes variety, good filter coffee and a limited range of cakes. In summer its open doors and location

at the edge of the flimsily fenced lake with its dramatic fountain can make it a bit of a nightmare with toddlers.

This side of the park has plenty of green spaces to run about in, plenty of scope for strolls through attractive landscaping, designated paved paths for cycling and some pretty areas including the Glade at the eastern tip of the lake, a semi-enclosed garden surrounded by shrubs that's a peaceful place to hang out with small children. But if it's size you're after, try the east side.

Walk past the grotesque Burdett-Coutts drinking fountain (1862) and what was originally a bathing lake but is now home to swans, ducks and Canada geese and you come to the Pools Playground. This has a fantastic central rocky mountain with terrifyingly high, narrow slides for over-7s and basic equipment for younger children, so it's a good place to come if you have both. The main attraction in summer is the sinuous paddling pool.

Beyond this is the one o'clock club and a generous enclosure housing half a dozen contented-looking deer. Beyond these is still more green space and trees, but at this point our legs gave out and we headed for home. vw

ADDRESS Grove Road, London E3 (020 8985 1957/020 8525 9416)
OPEN 7.00 to dusk
GETTING THERE Bethnal Green Underground; free car park on Grove Road

outdoor spaces

animals

Deen City Farm

If it weren't for city farms, many London children (including my own) would grow up in a world where the animals that feature so prominently in their books are the stuff of fantasy. Many of London's boroughs have excellent farms that involve the local communities in their running: College Farm (25 Fitzalan Road, London N3) has pretty Grade-II listed buildings including a blue-and-white tiled café where you can take tea on Sunday afternoons, if you don't mind sharing the space with a photograph of Margaret Thatcher; Freightliners Farm (Sheringham Road, London N7) packs a lot of animals into a relatively small space; Hackney City Farm (1a Goldsmiths Row, London E2) has a very smelly pig and a large meadow to race around in; Kentish Town City Farm (1 Cressfield Close, Grafton Road, London NW5), crammed into the leftover spaces between railway lines, specialises in horses. The three we have chosen here (see also pages 2.14 and 2.16) all offer something special, and all have fully operational cafés.

Deen City Farm, set up in 1994 on Bunce's Meadow, part of the Morden Hall estate leased from the National Trust, is a compact, well-organised outfit that goes out of its way to be child-friendly. The animal attractions include a Small Pets corner with rabbits, guinea pigs, ferrets and soft grey-and-black chinchillas, donkeys Noel and Liam, a very brown cow, a beautiful black Anglo-Nubian goat (Marty) with floppy black-and-white ears, several white-and-chocolate-brown Jacobs sheep which the farm is building up into a pedigree flock, and on one of our visits eight just-walking pink piglets wallowing in and around a muddy puddle. There are also hens, ducks, geese and a dazzling red, gold and blue golden pheasant with his drab female companion. The entrance is lined with logs to jump on and the first enclosure has a green tractor you can sit on. There are informative captions about individual animals and

breeds – did you know goats originated in China 10 million years ago, or that in medieval times geese herded on week-long journeys to market had their feet dipped in tar to stop them going lame? There are also pony rides (weekdays, 15.30–16.00; weekends, 12.00–13.00, 14.30–15.30; £1). The pleasant café serves all-day breakfast, drinks and sandwiches.

It's worth walking along the banks of the River Wandle to Merton Abbey Mills, now a crafts market. Home to a calico-printing works from 1742, the complex was leased in 1832 by Edmund Littler. His firm's finely detailed prints attracted the attention of Arthur Liberty, who took over the works in 1904, continuing production there until 1972. Liberty demolished many of the old buildings, replacing them with the arts-and-crafts-style workshops that stand today. Among the survivors from an earlier era are the eighteenth-century Colour House, now a theatre space with children's shows by in-house production company Wheelhouse at weekends at 14.00 and 16.00 (box office: 020 8542 6644), and the Wheel House, where you can still watch the huge waterwheel turning. On Sundays you can get platefuls of delicious and cheap Indonesian, Philippine, Caribbean or Thai food from stalls at the far end of the market; other food options include the William Morris Free House (Morris had workshops nearby from 1875), which has outside tables on its terrace and on the riverbank, and the twee Abbey Mills Gallery & Teahouse. On Sundays and Bank Holidays there's also a miniature steam train, the Lynton, that leaves from outside the pub. VW

ADDRESS 39 Windsor Avenue, London SW19 (020 8543 5300)
OPEN Tuesday to Sunday, 9.00–17.30
GETTING THERE Colliers Wood Underground; free car park

animals

London Aquarium

Those readers old enough to remember the heyday of Ken Livingstone's Greater London Council – in whose former headquarters, provocatively beaming London's unemployment statistics across the river to the Houses of Parliament, the London Aquarium is housed – are probably also familiar with the kind of trance-like drug-induced state watching the fish in their giant tanks engenders. Children love it too – the gasps of amazement that greet Karp (a flooded, fish-filled Ford Ka designed to make parting with the hefty entrance fee sweeter) echo throughout.

The most dramatic experiences are the double-height Atlantic and Pacific Ocean tanks. In addition to stingrays that dance along the floor and a central primitive-style sculpture, the Pacific tank has sharks – swift and graceful, in constant motion. From below you get a good view of the sand tiger sharks' toothy grins – despite their mean looks they're relatively docile and don't attack humans. The other highlight is the touch tanks: a large one where you can stroke the top of the rays and a smaller one in which you can pick up and hold hermit crabs, feathery plumose anemones and starfish. The Aquarium breeds some fish itself and occasionally you see tanks with shoals of babies and anxiously defensive parents.

At the end of the journey there's the shop – big and well stocked with information alongside the tat – and McDonald's where, whatever your politics, £1.99 for a meal, drink and toy is hard to resist. vw

ADDRESS County Hall, Westminster Bridge Road, London SE1 (020 7967 8000)
WEBSITE www.londonaquarium.co.uk
OPEN daily, 10.00–18.00
COST adults £8, concessions £6.50, 3s–14s £5, family ticket £22
GETTING THERE Waterloo Underground

London Zoo

'The OK thing to do, on Sunday afternoon, is to toddle in the Zoo.'
The Great Vance, Edwardian music-hall singer

London Zoo has got to be one of the top children's attractions in the capital. Here in the middle of the city are real-life elephants, bears, rhinos, monkeys, tigers, lions, giraffes, zebras – not to mention snakes, bugs, birds and fish, and less well-known creatures such as bush-tailed bettong and Arabian spiny mice. And as if this wasn't enough, they're housed in examples of late twentieth-century architecture that put some human dwellings to shame.

For first-time visitors, it can be hard to know where to start. Or, if you're a regular, it's all too easy simply to head for a few favourites – monkeys, elephants and the aquarium in our case – and leave other areas unexplored. It doesn't help that the zoo is in effect divided in two, with hoofed animals, the invertebrate house, small mammals (including Moonlight World, interesting if smelly) and the wonderful dramatically-sculpted Cedric Price/Lord Snowdon-designed Aviary separated from the rest by a road, Regent's Park Outer Circle.

It's a good idea to arm yourself at the main entrance with a map of the zoo and a list of the day's events (elephant weighing, snake feeding, 'Animals in Action' sessions in the amphitheatre and so on). Then, if you want to make sure you see the highlights, follow the green 'footprint trail' which begins at the tunnel near the main gate and continues past all the main exhibits. In a way, though, the joy of the zoo for children is that it's a clean and safe place in which they can run about, discovering the animals that interest them.

Inevitably, the zoo has its stars. The penguins (housed in Grade-I listed accommodation designed by Tecton and Berthold Lubetkin in 1934; try

to catch them at feeding time), elephants (in a building designed by Sir Hugh Casson in 1965), monkeys, bears and big cats are the Liz Taylors of the place. Less glitzy but also very popular are the endlessly patient goats of the Touch Paddock in the Children's Zoo – one of the latest architectural additions built with materials that conform with the World Wide Fund for Nature's guidelines – which good-naturedly let themselves be petted and pursued by streams of small children. Alongside is a pet-care centre, which explains how to take care of gerbils, rabbits, goldfish, hamsters and such like (and offers some good advice; for example think carefully before you are talked into buying a pet terrapin – they live for around 30 years and they smell).

Another of the big attractions is the Web of Life biodiversity exhibition. Opened in 1999, it introduces visitors to the astonishing range of life forms found in different habitats around the world. Here you can see naked mole rats scurrying around tunnels, seemingly caught without their clothes on; a huge, hairy red-knee spider; desert beetles' footprints in the sand; cockroaches, locusts, and leafcutter ants straight out of *A Bug's Life*. Children can look through a low-level magnifying glass to watch water fleas hopping about, they can peer through microscopes or hunt for the apple snail's bright pink eggs. It's a terrific exhibition. Leave your bug-phobias at the door and enjoy.

The aquarium, which runs under the Mappin Terraces, is beginning to show its age these days (especially compared to the new London Aquarium; see page 2.6), but its sharks, piranhas and beautifully coloured rainbow fish remain perennially popular.

There are frequent displays and animal encounters in the amphitheatre (near the fountains), and pony rides in Riding Square at certain times of the day.

Of course, the zoo has a lot going for it besides animals – carousel, shops and playgrounds, plus face-painting and bouncy castle in the summer months. It's even possible to book birthday parties at the zoo (contact Rampage on 020 7722 5909).

There are various food kiosks dotted around, and a self-service café next to the fountains which sells hot meals, jars of baby food, children's lunchboxes and so on. It can get extremely busy during peaktimes, so lunch early or late, or be prepared to queue. Alternatively, there are benches or green spaces where you can sit and picnic.

A trip to the zoo isn't cheap, but whatever age your children are it's easy to spend a very enjoyable day here. For us, membership of Lifewatch – which gives free admission, shop and café discounts, free parking at certain times, and two half-price guest tickets per year – has proved a good investment (annual membership for one adult and one child costs £43; for two adults and two children it costs £86). JL

ADDRESS Regent's Park, London NW1 (020 7722 3333)
WEBSITE www.zsl.org
OPEN daily, March to October, 10.00–17.30; November to February, 10.00–16.00 (last admission one hour before closing)
COST adults £9, concessions £8, 3s–14s £7
GETTING THERE Baker Street Underground; via waterbus (London Waterbus Company 020 7482 2660); pay-and-display parking on Regent's Park Outer Circle; there is also a coach and car park at Gloucester Gate (£15 per car with £10 refunded on entry to the zoo
BUGGIES/WHEELCHAIR ACCESS some areas; a map showing wheelchair/buggy access is available from the main gate or information kiosk

Mudchute Park and Farm

The area known as the Mudchute on the Isle of Dogs was created when the spoil and silt from the construction of Millwall Dock in the late nineteenth century was dumped on to nearby land. Over time this became a natural wilderness and a playground for local youngsters, though officially the site was closed to the public. In 1974 the area was earmarked by the GLC for the construction of a high-rise estate, but following a public campaign the site was secured as a 'people's park'. In 1977 the Mudchute Association was formed to preserve and develop it.

Sprawling in a surreal setting, Mudchute covers 13 hectares and feels less like a showpiece than any of the other farms we visited. A circular route takes you past two llamas, six breeds of goat including fluffy white Angora and floppy-eared Anglo-Nubians, sheep, several kinds of pig, horses, cows, ugly turkeys and hens. The circuit is a bit like a country ramble, and the spacious enclosures make you feel assured of the animals' welfare. There's also a Pets' Corner (open 10.00–16.00) with stripy chipmunks, smelly polecats, guinea pigs, rabbits and brightly coloured lovebirds, rosellas and cockatiels. Pony rides (£1.50) are available at weekends from 12.00–13.00 and on weekdays from 14.00–14.30, and you can watch experienced riders in the paddock for inspiration. The extremely cheap café, its walls lined with an exhibition of the history of the Isle of Dogs, serves burgers, nuggets, sandwiches and drinks. The highlight for us, however, was the meadow with its bizarrely shaped mounds and views of the Millennium Dome, Canary Wharf and other human follies. VW

ADDRESS Pier Street, Isle of Dogs, London E14 (020 7515 5901)
OPEN fields: unrestricted; farmyard: 9.00–17.00 summer; 10.00–16.00 winter
GETTING THERE Mudchute DLR

animals

Surrey Docks Farm

Established in 1975, Surrey Docks Farm offers beehives that produce 200 kilos of honey annually, an orchard with 25 types of tree including apple, apricot, pear, plum and quince, a vegetable garden planted with beetroot, cabbages, maize and pumpkins, a forge where you can watch a blacksmith at work on festivals and open days, and magnificent views of the river and the several silly housing schemes opposite. The farm itself, by contrast, boasts a Segal building – self-built (by farm workers and volunteers), ecologically friendly (softwood walls and turf roof) and energy-efficient (turf for insulation; wind power for lighting; south-facing glass corridor). This houses the slightly pricey café (samosas, crisps, fruit, cakes and drinks only), a room devoted to bee-keeping equipment and information and a yurt. As well as organising demonstrations for schools and drop-in arts and crafts and farming activities for accompanied children during the summer holidays, Surrey Docks also runs New Leaf, a training programme in gardening, cheese-making and bee-keeping for people with learning difficulties.

The farm is hands-on as well as right-on. Its centrepiece is a large sheep and goat enclosure into which you step at your peril – once the food (available from the café at 50p a bag) is finished, it's your clothes the animals turn to. You can also walk into the rabbit pen, surrounded by a fence decorated with metal animals and leaves that is just one of many examples of the blacksmith's work that decorate the farm, and stroke the rabbits – there's even a hutch big enough for a rabbit and small child to share. The animals, including the most enormous black pig I've ever seen, cows, a donkey, hens and ducks, are arranged around a circular route with plenty of incident; education officer Daphne Ferrigan is working on a golden trail of art features that will weave more adventure and stories into the site. Members of the local community are fully involved –

gardeners are welcome to help themselves from the compost heap and teenagers serve in the café – and if they don't come to the farm, the farm goes to them, taking the yurt into the Surrey Quays shopping complex and surrounding it with an enchanted garden with storytelling laid on.

For more country-in-the-city experience, nearby Russia Dock Woodland (off Redriff Road, SE16) is a small tract of wood sandwiched between an industrial estate and the man-made Stave Hill ecological park. Good for picnics, wildflowers and butterflies. VW

ADDRESS Rotherhithe Street, London SE16
(020 7231 1010)
OPEN Tuesday to Sunday, 10.00–13.00 and
14.00–17.00
GETTING THERE Surrey Quays Underground

trains, boats and planes

Docklands Light Railway

If you spend a lot of time on public transport, a trip on the Docklands Light Railway may not be your idea of fun. But what's good about these automatic trains is that they have no driver – children can sit at the front and pretend to be at the controls, while the track winds along in front of them.

From Bank or Tower Gateway tube, the DLR goes in three directions – to Stratford, Beckton or Island Gardens. The route through Docklands, past Canary Wharf, takes you via the office tower blocks, waterside cafés and busy building sites that signify the area's regeneration. You can combine a trip with a visit to Mudchute City Farm (see page 2.14) or go under the Thames to maritime Greenwich and the Cutty Sark (see pages 1.24 and 3.16) on the newly opened Lewisham link.

Alternatively, you can take the longer Beckton route, past City Airport. Along the way you'll have a terrific view of the Millennium Dome on the other side of the water. Go to the end of the line and you can catch a no. 101 bus from outside Beckton station to the East Ham Nature Reserve (020 8470 4525) in nearby Norman Road. Set in what was once one of London's largest churchyards, it now provides a home for wildlife: follow the nature trails and spot, among the gravestones, crickets, butterflies, birds and – if you're lucky – even foxes, lizards and frogs.

The DLR runs seven days a week. If you travel on a weekday you may need to oust besuited business people from the front seats. Be ruthless. JL

GETTING THERE Bank or Tower Gateway Underground and stations *en route* (customer services 020 7363 9700; 24-hour hotline 020 7918 4000)
WEBSITE www.dlr.co.uk
TICKETS all DLR, LT or London Underground tickets (except Carnet tickets) and travelcards valid for the relevant zones (1–4) can be used
BUGGIES not ideal

trains, boats and planes

Golden Hinde

Moored beside the Thames close to Southwark Cathedral, this is a meticulous reconstruction (made in 1973) of the ship in which Sir Francis Drake circumnavigated the globe in the late 1570s. It's quite small, but there's plenty – capstans, cannons, captain's cabin – to fire the imagination, particularly of any child obsessed by pirates. The costumed staff like to delight older children with lurid descriptions of keelhauling, or gory tales of gun decks painted red so that the blood wouldn't show …

Steepish steps or ladders lead up to the poop deck or fore deck, or down to the gun deck and the hold below. While small children can run around happily below deck, adults have to stoop to avoid hitting their heads – it's a good job your average Elizabethan crew member was only 1.6 metres tall.

As we walked up the gangplank for our first visit, we thought it would take about 15 minutes to 'do' the Golden Hinde; in fact it took an hour and the bribe of an ice cream to lure our companion back on shore.

This a popular venue for parties for children aged 4+ (our son had a great fourth birthday on board); the ship is therefore sometimes closed to the public, so telephone first to confirm opening times. 'Living History' workshops, including sleepovers, are also held on board. JL

ADDRESS St Mary Overie Dock, Cathedral Street, London SE1 (020 7403 0123; 08700 118700 for party/workshop details)
OPEN daily, 10.00–17.30 (telephone to confirm opening times)
GETTING THERE London Bridge Underground
COST adults £2.50, children £1.75, family ticket (two adults and up to three children) £6.50, concessions £2.10. Guided tours available
BUGGIES/WHEELCHAIR ACCESS no

HMS Belfast

Launched on St Patrick's Day 1938 and named after the city in which she was built, HMS Belfast served in both the Second World War and Korea, then in peacetime in the Far East, before being retired in the early 1960s. In 1971 she was brought to the Pool of London, where she is now run as a museum-ship, the last surviving example of the big-gun armoured warships built for the Royal Navy in the first half of the twentieth century.

Your trip around the Belfast involves lots (*lots*) of steep steps and ladders, so leave any buggies on the quarterdeck (this isn't a trip to attempt with toddlers, and even older children need to be fairly closely supervised). Head past the 14-inch guns, once used to protect the ship from attack by enemy aircraft, to the open space of the boatdeck from which reconnaissance seaplanes were launched by catapult early in the Second World War.

From here your tour is pretty thoroughly signposted, though it is difficult to visit the numbered zones in any kind of sensible order if your children are, like mine, running around over-excited by such things as the 40mm Bofors guns which visitors can crank up or down. Overlooking the fo'c'sle are more big gun turrets, these ones apparently trained on the Scratchwood motorway services area more than 12 miles away (something to think about next time you're driving along the M1).

Below deck, mannequins and mock-up scenarios reconstruct key moments from the Second World War and – though rather cheesy – create a vivid picture of what life was like for the 950 or so crew jampacked on board: in the operations room, displays show sailors wearing anti-flash hoods to protect them from the burns that could result from an enemy shell exploding on the bridge; in the compass platform, sound effects reconstruct the Belfast's role in the Battle of North Cape in 1943 ('Fire 1! Fire 2! Give it everything you've got!'). It's exciting stuff for chil-

dren – and seemingly for grown men too – though it also tells a sobering story about the realities of war at sea. Elsewhere more everyday scenes are depicted: the captain in his cabin, sailors playing dominos or drinking 'ky' (cocoa). Later on during the tour, in Zone 7, you can see how HMS Belfast looked towards the end of her seafaring life, after a modernising refit. Look out for the ship's cat, busy catching rats in the potato store.

Last stop on the tour is the boiler room, but the way down – a daunting network of ladders and pipework – is only for the very sure-footed.

The Walrus Café, near the boatdeck, offers a standard selection of rolls, ice creams, lunchboxes, teas and so on.

Before you leave via the quarterdeck, take a look at the ship's silver bell: given by the people of Belfast in 1948, it was used upturned as a font, and inside its rim are the names of all the children born and christened on board. The way-out takes you via the museum shop.

On-board birthday parties can be arranged, when children can not only see the ship but also try on uniforms, climb into hammocks and so on (prices start at £8 per child). JL

ADDRESS Morgans Lane, Tooley Street, London SE1 (020 7940 6300)
WEBSITE www.hmsbelfast.org.uk
OPEN Monday to Sunday, 10.00–18.00 (last admission 17.15) from 1 March to 31 October (closes one hour earlier from 1 November to 28 February)
COST adults £4.70, concessions £3.60, disabled £2.35, under-16s free (prices due to increase end March 2000)
GETTING THERE Tower Hill Underground
BUGGIES no WHEELCHAIR ACCESS to quarterdeck and limited other areas; telephone prior to visit to arrange assistance

Jason's Canal Boat Trip

The exciting thing about a narrow boat is that you feel alarmingly close to the dirty water and the ducks, coots, Canada geese and Coke cans that float by. The 45-minute trip on Jason's runs from Little Venice to Camden Lock. The live commentary by a former boatman was personal (we saw the hospital where his six-week-old baby was born), political (digs at greedy developers), patronising ('bow – that's the sharp end at the front') and genuinely funny ('it's a sectionable offence to talk to strangers in London, but on the canals it's more friendly') as well as informative. Along the way we passed the island where Robert Browning had a summer house, the pleasantly scary 250-metre-long Maida Hill tunnel, £8 million houses cheek by jowl with council developments, and the dramatic aviary designed by Lord Snowdon and Cedric Price for London Zoo (see page 2.8).

If you want to eat at Camden Lock and take a later boat back try the café where you disembark or JinJoks opposite for superior sandwiches and salads. The market is a treasure trove of ethnic clothes, crafts and jewellery; shops with appeal for children include Kate's Corner for dolls' houses and furniture, Joka for masks, Village Games, the Beanie Babies stall in front of JinJoks and Paint Me Pottery, which offers a similar deal to Art 4 Fun (see page 7.2). VW

ADDRESS Jason's Wharf, opposite 60 Blomfield Road, London W9 (020 7286 3428)
DEPARTURES daily, 10.30, 12.30, 14.30; extra boats: April to September weekends and bank holidays 16.30; May and June weekends 11.30, 13.30, 15.30
COST £5.95 return, £4.95 single; under-14s £4.50/£3.75; under-3s free
GETTING THERE Warwick Avenue Underground

trains, boats and planes

London Transport Museum

Housed in a light and airy building, once part of Covent Garden's fruit and vegetable market, this is one of our favourite museums. Telling the story of London's public transport from the first omnibus right up to the present day, it is accessible and informative, and makes every effort to make its subject-matter fun for children.

As well as the gleaming horse buses, trolleybuses, trains and trams (some of which visitors can board), there is plenty of hands-on stuff, such as tube simulators (try your hand as a driver) or signals to switch on. Most notable are the 'KidZones' – 15 big, bright displays explaining notions such as horse power, or how much energy is needed to move a tram compared to a trolleybus, all the while encouraging lots of handle turning, button pushing and bell dinging. At each one children can punch their special KidZones ticket.

Also popular with small children is the Funbus (ground floor behind the motor buses) which has bells, buttons and wheels for the under-5s, and softplay cushions for those 18 months and under. But children know the real thing when they see it, and the most sought after (and fought over) hands-on display is the front section of a 1993 'Hoppa' bus (upstairs to the right of the resource centre). Here they can sit in a real bus-driver's seat, twiddle real indicators and, if they can reach, step on real pedals. Special activities for children are arranged during school holidays – telephone the museum for details.

Well-designed panels, videos and touch-screen displays give more detailed information about London's transport. But if children find these too hard-going they'll still be fascinated by snippets such as the fact that in 1900 the capital's buses and trams relied on 50,000 horses, resulting in traffic chaos and some 1000 tonnes of dung daily. Archive photographs give glimpses of everyday life in a now unrecognisable London.

London Transport Museum

Throughout the museum, display cases – some of them low enough for very small children to peer into – hold detailed models of carriages or coaches, or maybe a mini Docklands Light Railway train arriving at and departing from Mudchute station. A favourite of ours is the case showing the building of the Metropolitan railway in the 1860s: look through the peepholes to glimpse steam cranes, wooden scaffolding, horses pulling cartloads of earth, men digging with shovels, and well-dressed ladies picking their way gingerly across the disrupted streets.

There are also examples of posters which remind you just what a great patron of design London Transport has been. Don't miss the Frank Pick gallery (named after the man who built up LT's design identity) or the Harry Beck room, near the exit, which explains just why the tube map he came up with in the 1930s is now considered such a design classic.

The exit is via the museum shop, which has an imaginative selection of themed souvenirs. Next to the shop is an Aroma café (sit upstairs if you can to enjoy a view down over the museum). There are plenty of places nearby to eat more substantially, including the ever child-friendly TGI Friday in Bedford Street and Smollensky's on the Strand (see page 9.6). For shopping in Covent Garden, see page 10.8. JL

ADDRESS Covent Garden Piazza, London WC2 (020 7379 6344; recorded information 020 7565 7299)
WEBSITE www.ltmuseum.co.uk
OPEN daily, 10.00–18.00 (except Friday, 11.00–18.00), last admission 17.15
COST adults £5.50, children £2.95, under-5s free, concessions £2.95, family ticket (two adults, two children) £13.90, family season ticket £24
GETTING THERE Covent Garden Underground

National Maritime Museum

This, the world's largest maritime museum, was a favourite even before the recent £20 million redevelopment programme. Since the opening of a new Lottery-funded wing in May 1999, it houses 20 galleries devoted to ships and seafaring which provide plenty for children to see and do. One imagines a few old seadogs shaking their heads at the new-fangled zippiness of it all – themed spaces and a few rather tacky displays – but for children and families it's a hugely enjoyable museum. With Greenwich Park on the doorstep (see page 1.22) and an excellent ship-shaped climbing frame at the back of the museum, it's easy to spend the whole day here.

At the main entrance you are met by images flashing across a giant video screen and the roar of waves (transmitted live via ISDN from Chesil Beach). Pick up a free copy of the Nelson or Treasures family trail here if you want to, and head into the light, bright, glass-roofed space.

Large-scale exhibits – such as the optic from the Tarbat Ness lighthouse, a vast propeller, and Prince Frederick's golden barge – are displayed along a series of 'streets' on the ground floor. Here too is a warren of small themed galleries into which children can dip and dive. The Explorers galleries, for instance, feature simulated shipwrecks with flickering footage of the Titanic salvage operations, or 'icy' caves echoing to the sound of gusting winds and creaking rigging. There's also a navigation room, where small lights in the ceiling are reflected in mirrored walls to create a magical, starry space. Rank & Style shows changing naval dress codes, from the trend-setting sailor suit worn by Edward VII as a young prince, to sealskin outfits used for Arctic expeditions. Open locker doors to look at them – but watch out for tiny fingers, and even heads (we've seen some children try to shut themselves in the lockers). The Passengers gallery, meanwhile, is full of ship models and displays

which show what life was like on the liners of the nineteenth and early twentieth centuries, contrasting the luxury of first-class travellers (marble fireplaces, electric radiators, drawing rooms, etc) with the eight-to-a-cabin squeeze of steerage. Another wonderful ship's model is the Endeavour, upstairs in the Global Garden, which shows in tiny, fascinating detail the crew – including a carpenter, armourer, sailmaker, musician, surgeon, astronomer and artist – who went in search of exotic plants and natural resources in the eighteenth century (try to spot Captain Cook).

For children, the fun really starts at the interactive Bridge and All Hands galleries. The former is officially aimed at 7- to 11-year-olds, though younger children can enjoy a lot of what's on offer, while the latter has something for just about everyone. Children will find plenty to get stuck into in these two galleries: they can, for example, send Morse code signals, pull up flags or grope around in thick rubber gloves to see what it's like being a diver in murky water. Or they can try their hand at the wheel of a paddle steamer or rowing a Viking ship, operate a crane to load cargo, or aim cannon. Both galleries are very popular, with queues at busy times, and it's not unknown for children to have to be dragged off the crane or the cannon kicking and screaming. Shipmates drop-in workshops are held in the All Hands gallery on most Saturdays from 14.00 to 16.00 for children aged 7 and up. For younger children, the Crowsnest Club runs occasional story and game sessions.

Computer-loving children will also enjoy the multimedia databases in the excellent Search Station (tucked away on level 2). Try the Trade & Empire quiz which is especially good for children: get a correct answer and an animated ship proceeds on its journey across the screen, a wrong one and it starts to sink.

trains, boats and planes

What with all this child-friendly stuff, it's easy to miss the museum's more traditional galleries. But the Seapower gallery, dominated by a model of a ship's hull and an A-class submarine, is well worth a visit: the warship simulator systems, which involve lots of sonar and bleeps and buttons, are always very popular, and the works by war artists such as Sir Muirhead Bone and Barnett Freedman are quite wonderful. There is also a gallery devoted to Nelson.

The Neptune Court Café on level 2 has cakes, coffees, sandwiches and so on, and room for children to run around; the Bosun's Whistle Restaurant, which sells more substantial fare, is also on level 2, on the Greenwich Park side of the museum (there is outside seating for fine days). Both sell children's pirate-ship lunchboxes. The main shop is next to the entrance.

Before you leave, take a look at the dozen or so anchors – some of them huge and gnarled – on the eastern side of the grounds, or simply enjoy the views through columned walkways to Greenwich Park and the Observatory beyond. JL

ADDRESS Romney Road, London SE10 (020 8858 4422; information line 020 8312 6565)
WEBSITE www.nmm.ac.uk
OPEN daily, 10.00–17.00 (last admission 16.30)
COST adults £7.50, children free, concessions £6 (combined entry to Maritime Museum and Royal Observatory: adults £10.50, children free, concessions £8.40). For regular visitors, the £28 family friends membership is very good value
GETTING THERE Greenwich rail; DLR to Cutty Sark; riverboat from Westminster, Charing Cross or Tower; parking in Greenwich is generally difficult

North Woolwich Old Station Museum

This is a terrific little museum, lovingly run, beautifully kept – and free.

Housed in the Italianate station which opened in 1847 to connect the then bustling town of North Woolwich with the City, it contains photographs, documents, models and other objects relating to the history of the Great Eastern Railway (later the LNER) and the people who worked on it. Displayed in the old booking hall, ticket office and waiting rooms are station signs, vending machines (for example for Amplex deodorant tablets which 'banish odours on breath and body' for only 6d), and some wonderful railway posters. There are also some simple but effective interactive displays which allow children to load up a ship with a Meccano crane, build a bridge (see if it stands up when you take away the keystone) or level the ground to lay a railway line. Quiz sheets are available for under- or over-8s (and a lollipop when they complete it). Special activities are arranged for children during the school holidays.

Outside are engines, coaches and wagons, including the 1870s 'Coffee Pot' locomotive which stands on what was once the station turntable, an 1870s luggage van with ventilated dog boxes, and Dudley the Diesel. And if you don't mind the heat of the furnace, you can climb into the driver's cab of the rather wheezy Peckett as it chugs a short distance along the track. It is only in steam on the first Sunday of each month, so this is the best time to visit (and because it is staffed by volunteers, you should telephone to check it will be running before you set out).

Teas, coffees, juices and delicious home-made cakes are sold on the station platform on steam days, served in GER cups and plates. When we visited on a baking hot August day, free cups of chilled water were also available. There is a small shop selling mostly inexpensive toys and souvenirs. The toilets, next to the waiting rooms, are spotlessly clean (though the hard toilet paper is perhaps taking nostalgia too far!).

trains, boats and planes

North Woolwich Old Station Museum

If you come by train, you'll arrive on the platform right next to the museum. If you're coming from south of the river, you can take the foot tunnel or the Woolwich free ferry (see page 7.22) which lands you just outside the Museum and gives you a great view of the Thames Barrier *en route*. JL

ADDRESS Pier Road, North Woolwich, London E16 (020 7474 7244)
OPEN January to November, Saturday and Sunday 13.00–17.00, plus Monday to Wednesday 13.00–17.00 during Newham school holidays. Closed December. Telephone to check opening times and details for steam days before setting out
GETTING THERE North Woolwich rail or from Woolwich via ferry or foot tunnel

trains, boats and planes

Original London Sightseeing Tour

A sightseeing tour by bus is first of all a sensual experience – the heady pleasure of sitting high up, 'with the warm wind in her hair' as Marianne Faithfull memorably described a never-to-be-had ride through Paris, watching London and the world go by. It inverts the usual London motoring equation: here, the heavier the traffic, the more enjoyable the ride. And you escape the heavy policing of most London buses – as long as the top deck is relatively empty, you and your children are free to run up and down, swap seats to get a better view and make as much noise as you want.

Unless you want to go to Madame Tussaud's, we'd recommend the Language Tour, whose two-hour circuit takes in Hyde Park Corner, Marble Arch, Piccadilly Circus, Trafalgar Square, Whitehall, Parliament Square, St Paul's, Tower Bridge and Victoria Embankment. Buses run every 5 to 15 minutes and you can get on or off at any stop as often as you want in the course of a day. Both tours offer Kids Club commentary, in which Jack and Lucy discuss the passing sights. An activity pack and pens are also supplied.

You'll be surprised how much you can see: the position and slow pace enable you to appreciate the magical view down Whitehall from Parliament Square, the delicacy of the gothic tracery on the Houses of Parliament and Big Ben, the detail of the mouldings on the Banqueting House, the drama of the two huge naked women who guard the doorway of the Ministry of Defence. The route takes in six bridges: for us London Bridge with its view of Tower Bridge and HMS Belfast was the biggest thrill, though the ten minutes stuck in traffic on Lambeth Bridge with views of the Houses of Parliament and Lambeth Palace was no mean pleasure.

The taped commentary, aimed at tourists (many of whom were asleep), can sound obvious but is nevertheless crammed with informa-

trains, boats and planes

tion. Did you know it's illegal to sing, hum or whistle in the Burlington Arcade, or that King George III bought Buckingham Palace for £28,000 in 1762, or that both John Kennedy and Mick Jagger attended the LSE? There's an attempt to give a socio-economic perspective alongside the shopping information and copious references to Diana, Princess of Wales. County Hall is described as the former home of the GLC, 'abolished by Margaret Thatcher's government' rather than just the home of the London Aquarium; Mayfair (named – did you know? – after the May fairs stopped in 1764 after complaints from residents as the area became more upmarket) is presented as an exclusive playground for the rich, a world at which we, the sightseers, can only stop and stare, with the emphasis on the £200-a-time hairdresser, Rolls Royce showroom and Ritz Hotel.

The Kids Club commentary has Jack telling Lucy about his favourite painting in the National Gallery, and the large number of horses on the streets of London in Victorian times – 'think of the manure!' Unfortunately the relationship is a bit of an elder brother/younger sister affair, with Jack giving most of the facts and Lucy asking leading questions, or Jack correcting her information and putting her down (though she does have her moments, insisting, for instance, that girls too attended school). The tape machines are not all reliable, and Kids Club commentary is not available from every seat – in which case, sit back and enjoy the view. vw

INFORMATION 020 8877 1722
WEBSITE www.TheOriginalTour.com
COST adults £12.50, children £7.50, under-5s free

RAF Museum

The RAF Museum is housed in two surviving hangars on the site of the old Hendon aerodrome, once the site of annual air displays and a wartime airfield for transport aircraft. The museum tells the story of aviation from its earliest days, explaining the development of the Royal Air Force along the way.

Inevitably, many of the most impressive exhibits date from the Second World War, when the RAF was regarded as the 'thin blue line' defending Britain – there is, for example, a Lancaster bomber that flew 137 missions, a Spitfire and a Sunderland flying boat which visitors can walk through. There is also an American Flying Fortress. All pretty imposing for those of us who have only ever seen this kind of thing in Kenneth More movies – close up to the planes you get a real sense of their scale.

For children, a favourite exhibit is the 'touch & try' Jet Provost cockpit which they can clamber into, twiddling levers and knobs to turn tailfins and ailerons. This is in the Main Aircraft Hall, where you'll also find the flight simulator: for £1.50 a ride, children 1 metre or taller can get a taste of flying in a Tornado on a low-level training mission.

Don't miss the Fun 'n' Flight gallery, which has plenty more hands-on exhibits aimed at teaching 6- to 12-year-olds the basics of flight: here you can, for example, measure windspeed, 'fly' a model plane, or land a miniature food parcel into a drop zone (this was my son's favourite – we spent so long on it that we were eventually chivvied off by a sixty-something anxious for his turn).

During the school holidays the museum arranges children's activities such as rocket workshops, hot-air balloon week or evacuee experiences. In addition there are daily 'Plane & Simple' demonstrations – rather endearingly given with the help of a vacuum cleaner and a few props – which explain the principles of flight.

trains, boats and planes

Since the museum isn't exactly handy for restaurants, the choice is to picnic outside or eat at the Engine Bay Café in the Main Aircraft Hall, or the Wings Restaurant next to the Battle of Britain Hall which sells decent hot food in dreary surroundings. Decor-wise, the museum shop has been untouched by the retail revolution, but has a good selection of inexpensive souvenirs as well as larger items such as flying jackets. JL

ADDRESS Grahame Park Way, London NW9 (020 8205 2266; information line 0891 6005 633)
WEBSITE www.rafmuseum.org.uk
OPEN daily, 10.00–18.00
COST adults £6.50, children £3.25, OAPS £4.90, under-5s free (standard tickets allow free return visit within six months)
GETTING THERE Colindale Underground or Mill Hill Broadway rail then approximately 15-minute walk; bus 303 passes right in front of the museum; signposted from North Circular, M1, A41 and A5; ample free parking
WHEELCHAIR ACCESS not to Sunderland flying boat

museums and galleries

BBC Experience

Tickets for the BBC Experience are sold on a timed-tour basis and it's best to pre-book by telephone to avoid, as they say, disappointment. The first time we visited – or tried to visit – we queued for 15 minutes before being told that the next available tour was not for another four hours. We were so cross we nearly didn't return, but in the end were glad we did. For the over-5s, it's a very enjoyable look at behind-the-scenes Beeb.

Sandwiched between a film presentation and a medley of archive clips (not much fun for young children), you get the chance to help record a radio drama. This involves making sound effects, reading the lines from a short play (we did a spooky vampire drama) or, for younger ones, simply sitting at consoles and happily pressing buttons to produce the sounds of creaking doors, organ music, flapping bats' wings and so on.

After your tour you are released into the main exhibition space which is full of interactive opportunities: you can be Sue Lawley's guest on *Desert Island Discs*, animate Badger and Mouse puppets, edit a scene from *EastEnders*, have a go at being a sports commentator or present the weather forecast with the help of an on-screen Bill Giles. Allow one and a half to two hours for your visit.

The way out is via the BBC Shop which sells Beeb-related souvenirs, books and videos of programmes old and new. Alongside is a café. JL

ADDRESS Broadcasting House, Portland Place, London W1 (0870 603 0304)
WEBSITE www.bbc.co.uk/experience
OPEN Tuesday to Sunday, 10.00–18.00; Monday, 11.00–18.00. Last tour 16.30
COST adults £6.95, children £4.95. Family tickets available
GETTING THERE Oxford Circus Underground
BUGGIES no WHEELCHAIR ACCESS telephone in advance

Bethnal Green Museum of Childhood

This treasure trove of a museum has enough exhibits and activities to keep children entertained for an afternoon at least.

The ground floor is devoted to dolls' houses. It's probably better to look closely at one or two than to try to take in them all: I'd recommend the enormous Dingley Hall (1874, near the entrance on the left), a fantastic mansion inhabited by some 20 soldiers retired from various regiments and including a chapel with two priests of different denominations, four rooms set for tea and a nursery crowded with eight children and their toys. 3 Devonshire Villas (half way along on the left) is a recreation of a real house (now 389 Kilburn High Road) made in 1900 by Samuel Loebe for his daughter. Curb your children's social aspirations as you enjoy the wonderful detail of the huge kitchen and the nursery crammed with playthings including an early baby-walker. Adults might be amused by the 1960s teenage bedroom in Mrs Hibberd's House (on the right near the café) with its pink satin sofa, guitar and empty wine bottles.

The gallery on the right has two model railways (one with Thomas, Annie and Clarabel) and a rocking horse children can ride on alongside cars, ships, teddy bears, Noah's arks and a beach buggy designed by De Stijl architect Gerrit Rietveld. You'll need a supply of 20p coins to operate the railways and model dodgem track. The gallery on the left has an overwhelming collection of dolls which no child I've taken to the museum has shown the slightest interest in – it's much more fun (and worrying to parents) to play hide and seek among the angled display cabinets. Obsessive small boys might enjoy the toy soldiers.

The top floor is much more relaxed and spacious than downstairs. On one side are displays of Learning Toys and Let's Pretend Toys including a terrifying array of children's sewing machines from the early twentieth century and tiny typewriters from the 1930s. There are also hands-on toys

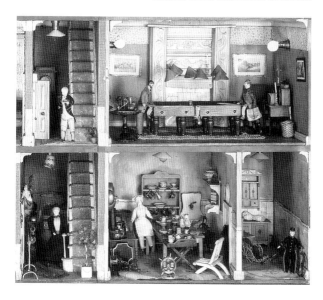

including full-height blackboards and chalk, a giant abacus and a selection of wire-and-bead puzzles. On the other side is an exhibition of clothing, with shoes and hats from down the ages that children can try on. Small girls might be horrified by the display of Henrietta Byron's restrictive nightclothes and underwear from 1840 and boys by the fact that in the eighteenth and nineteenth centuries young males wore dresses until the age of 6 when they were presented with their first pair of trousers in a breeching ceremony. Alongside an unadventurous showcase of green, red and gold Rastafarian clothing – a half-hearted attempt to get away from the white middle-class bias of the rest of the artefacts – is a disturbing Self-Discovery case which attempts to illustrate the tortured process of female adolescent sexual awakening through bras and girdles (remember them?), teen magazines, love letters to the Beatles, a female razor and a selection of condoms.

The ground-floor café serves only sandwiches, salads and cakes and inadequate children's lunchboxes where the lunch element consists of a finger roll. However, it contains boxes of books and construction toys so you may be able to linger for some time. Outside is a relatively spacious green area with picnic tables – you can take time out here between looking at the displays. The museum organises creative art workshops for over-3s (free, admission by ticket available on the day) and holiday events. vw

ADDRESS Cambridge Heath Road, London E2 (020 8980 2415)
OPEN Monday to Thursday, Saturday and Sunday, 10.00–17.50
GETTING THERE Bethnal Green Underground

British Library

OK, the British Library isn't somewhere you'd take the kids for a day out – but it has a surprising amount for children, particularly the over-5s, to see and enjoy.

The Library moved to its controversial new home – the largest publicly funded building constructed in the UK in the twentieth century – in 1998. Just a few steps from noisy, traffic-laden Euston Road, it is approached via a spacious and pleasantly peaceful courtyard presided over by Eduardo Paolozzi's statue of Isaac Newton. Stop here if the weather's fine and enjoy an ice cream from the kiosk or a (rather good) coffee from the Chapter Coffee House. There's plenty of space here for children to burn off some energy before you head for the slightly hushed and reverential atmosphere of the Library itself.

Once inside, take a look at the King's Library – an impressive glass-walled six-storey tower of books in the centre of the building – then head for the three galleries open to the public.

The John Ritblat Gallery displays some of the treasures of the British Library, from the Magna Carta to Captain Scott's diary. For us, a highlight here are the headphones on which you can listen to some fascinating recordings from the British Library's National Sound Archive – everything from the voice of Florence Nightingale and an eye-witness account of the sinking of the Titanic to Bob Geldof talking about Live Aid. We also like the maps – some of them dating back as far as the eighth century: there are maps with pictures of ships, castles or horses, maps shaped like lions, even the earliest 'realistic' map from 1050. Check out too Turning the Pages, a computer-based interactive display on which you can explore some of the Library's most valuable items: touch the on-screen picture of, say, the Sforza Hours or the Lindisfarne Gospels to turn the pages, zooming in on details or listening to the audio accompaniment. In the

case of the Leonardo Notebook, you can even use the mirror button to reverse his characteristic mirror writing.

Next head downstairs for the Pearson Gallery of Living Words, which houses changing exhibitions. Past displays have included, for example, 'The Story of Writing', 'The Scientific Record', 'Images of Britain' and 'Children's Books'. A look at the work of Janet and Allan Ahlberg was accompanied by a free Jolly Postman quiz sheet when we visited.

The adjoining Workshop of Words, Sounds and Images offers a hands-on explanation of how books are made – from the methods of a fifteenth-century scribe to hot metal and the latest printing technology. On Saturdays the Workshop has regular demonstrations of hot-metal printing, calligraphy, bookbinding and so on (details from Visitor Services on 020 7412 7332).

The Library has a restaurant on the first floor serving English breakfasts, lunches and afternoon teas, and a café downstairs for cakes, pastries, sandwiches and other snacks (though they are both too calm and well behaved for our tastes). In the main hall next to the entrance is a bookshop selling a small selection of children's books. JL

ADDRESS 96 Euston Road, London NW1 (020 7412 7332 for visitor services)
WEBSITE www.bl.uk
OPEN Monday, Wednesday to Friday, 9.30–18.00; Tuesday, 9.30–20.00; Saturday, 9.30–17.00; Sunday and bank holidays, 11.00–17.00
GETTING THERE Euston rail or Underground
BUGGIES yes, can be left in locker room

British Museum

If it's hands-on, interactive fun you're after, the British Museum isn't for you. But though rather dry, it's packed with such an astonishing range of artefacts that it's hard not to find something to fascinate children, certainly the over-5s. Moreover, at the time of writing, the museum was embarked on 'one of the most important construction projects in its history' – the glass-roofed Norman Foster-designed Great Court. Opening in autumn 2000, this new public space promises improved facilities for visitors, including a centre for education, a café and galleries.

It's best either to pick up a free family quiz sheet or children's trail from the information desk at the entrance, or target a particular area. The Egyptian rooms are usually a good bet, since many children seem strangely fascinated by mummies and pyramids. Older children (with strong stomachs) also relish the displays of human remains such as the 2000-year-old Lindow Man.

The stairs and throngs of tourists mean that the British Museum isn't a great place to be with a buggy. The children's shop sells an imaginative selection of books, small toys and activity packs. The restaurant is a very civilised place to eat – too civilised for us, actually. We prefer the always child-friendly PizzaExpress in nearby Coptic Street (020 7636 3232). JL

ADDRESS Great Russell Street, London WC1 (020 7636 1555)
WEBSITE www.british-museum.ac.uk
OPEN Monday to Saturday, 10.00–17.00; Sunday, 12.00–18.00
COST free, though a minimum donation of £2 is suggested
GETTING THERE Tottenham Court Road Underground
BUGGIES yes – though it's best to leave them behind WHEELCHAIR ACCESS yes; recorded information for disabled visitors on 020 7637 7384

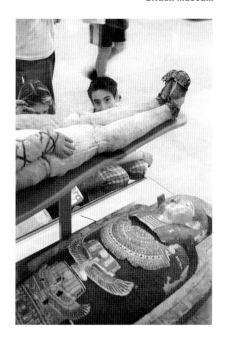

Cabaret Mechanical Theatre

Like a pantomime, this tiny museum operates on two levels: children enjoy the interaction of pressing the buttons and watching the spectacle; adults relish the sexual innuendo and wry wit.

Don't be misled by the crude models on display outside, where you can have your foot massaged or help Freddie swat a fly. Inside are some 60 more intricate and intelligent automata collected by Sue Jackson, who opened the museum in 1984. My favourites are by Paul Spooner, in particular the series of figures with the jackal head of the Egyptian god Anubis. The absurdity of the four Anubis-headed musclemen doing sit-ups, Australia's Topsy-Turvy Creatures No. 17: The Hopping Jackal – an Anubis-headed kangaroo reduced through overcrowding to skipping on the spot – or the Anubis highland chieftain watching his jackal-headed dog chase a sheep, is hard to beat. Also don't miss Hungry for Love, which has a sailor on his first night ashore waving his knife and fork as his woman, dressed in a waitress uniform, scurries up with a trolley with two breast-shaped plates which she opens to reveal enormous nipple-like pink jellies, or Manet's Olympia, who moves seductively while Anubis (replacing the flower-bearing black servant of the original) serves her Camp coffee, his hands trembling with anticipation … vw

ADDRESS 33/34 The Market, Covent Garden, London WC2 (020 7379 7961)
WEBSITE www.cabaret.co.uk
OPEN Monday to Saturday, 10.00–18.30; Sunday, 11.00–18.30
COST adults £1.95, concessions £1.20, under-5s free, family ticket £4.95
GETTING THERE Covent Garden Underground
BUGGIES/WHEELCHAIR ACCESS yes, once inside, but to reach the unit involves a flight of stairs; stools available for small children to stand on

Geffrye Museum

Housed in almshouses founded in 1714 with money left to the Ironmongers' Company by wealthy merchant Sir Robert Geffrye, this museum provides snapshots of middle-class life from 1600 to the present day through a series of carefully recreated room settings. We liked the mid seventeenth-century cradle with an eye carved into it to protect the baby from ill-fortune in the first room, the stuffed armadillo in the Stuart Room, the wig stand in the Early Georgian Room, the Grandfather clock in the Late Georgian Room and the entire blue Regency Room with its dominoes, chess set, harp and magnificent sofa and footstool. Captions are informative and well presented, and children can enjoy the dolls'-house-style cutaways of buildings with descriptions of construction, what went on where, and toilet arrangements (the privy in the seventeenth-century townhouse is sliced in two to reveal a surprised occupant). The series is interrupted by a chapel and a relaxed gallery cum reading room with comfy chairs, a library of books on interior design through the ages and a table strewn with recent magazines. My daughter was fascinated by the paintings of Victorian children playing tug of war, oranges and lemons and skipping.

A new wing designed by Nigel Coates (one of the architects of the Body Zone in the Millennium Dome, see page 6.4) houses twentieth-century design, special exhibitions and a light, spacious café serving bangers and mash, bagels, salads, sandwiches and cakes. The recreation of a 1990s loft – its living space containing *Captain Corelli's Mandolin*, Richard Rogers' *Cities* book, the *Guardian* 'Space' magazine and a copy of the *Economist* with a picture of Bill Clinton and the coverline 'Oh lucky man', its kitchen little other than an empty bottle of Evian water, a packet of Café Direct and a bottle of designer olive oil – illustrates the wit and attention to detail that have gone into the enterprise. Down the child-friendly

spiral staircase (there's a lift for buggies) is the Design Centre, which displays work for sale by contemporary Hackney craftspeople, and a selection of twentieth-century tableware. My daughter enjoyed our reminiscences of which family friends had once owned what, from the plaid tea sets of the mid 1950s to the once-trendy Sun Moon and Earth of the 1970s, remnants of which are still lurking in the cupboard. Also on display are photographs and work from the workshops the museum runs in school holidays.

An area upstairs houses touch-screen computers with century-by-century information on furniture and domestic life illustrated through photographs of objects and paintings. There is intelligent text for older children and adults while young children can enjoy choosing icons from the quick-find menu, scrolling through the pages and selecting details for enlargement. The herb garden and series of period gardens corresponding to the spaces inside (open April to October) are more outdoor rooms than places to play. They were only established in 1999, so it will be interesting to watch them grow over the years.

The museum presents a much plusher view of English life than is indicated by the almshouses that accommodate it and gives little impression of the history (see Victoria Park, page 1.44) or present reality of the area in which it is located. vw

ADDRESS Kingsland Road, London E2 (020 7739 9893)
OPEN Tuesday to Saturday, 10.00–17.00; Sundays and bank holidays, 14.00–17.00
GETTING THERE Old Street Underground then short walk or bus 243; free parking on side streets

Horniman Museum

A weird but rather wonderful museum, and free, too. It was founded at the turn of the century to house the varied collections of Frederick Horniman, tea merchant, naturalist, MP, and apparently so voracious a collector that even as a child he stuffed treasures under his bed.

The heart of the museum is the natural-history collection, a menagerie of stuffed creatures such as squirrels, bats, badgers, bugs, monkeys and – most spectacularly – a vast walrus. All but the walrus are housed in old-fashioned glass cases which add considerably to the museum's odd charm, though for some children a number of the displays – pickled mouse embryos, for instance – might be a bit too much.

For us, a favourite feature of the museum is its aquarium, which has a range of fish and other creatures (the seahorses being particularly popular) in low-level tanks which descend the stairway and which are perfect for small children to press their noses against.

African Worlds is housed in the restored south hall – more stylish but less endearing than the main galleries. It contains masks, sculptures, headdresses, plaques and other ancestral objects chosen from the Horniman collection by curators from Nigeria, Trinidad and the UK. Alongside are comments about them from members of black communities from both this country and Africa. The cultural complexity of these objects may be lost on small children but their visual drama won't go unappreciated.

The museum organises a varied programme of workshops for children and families, most of which must be booked in advance.

Sadly, both the Centre for Understanding the Environment (one of the museum's most child-friendly galleries) and the music room will be closed during 2000 and 2001 as an ambitious development programme gets under way. An impressive new wing is being built, designed by architects Allies and Morrison and funded by Lottery money. It will house a new

anthropological gallery, an improved music room (the museum's collection includes more than 6000 musical instruments, from flutes and lutes to spike fiddles and frame drums), a temporary exhibition space and a bigger, better shop and café. (There will, however, be virtual access to 1000 instruments from the music collection during construction via the museum's website.) A new ramped entrance and lift access should help to make life easier for visitors with buggies or wheelchairs. There are also plans to link the gardens and museums as Frederick Horniman intended when he gave the building to the local community in 1901. Inevitably all this will mean considerable disruption (and very limited refreshment facilities) at the Horniman, lasting probably well into 2002, but this delightful, unusual museum is well worth putting up with a bit of scaffolding, dustsheets and upheaval.

The museum gardens are worth a visit too, with fine views over London. Here you'll find a small animal enclosure, a bandstand with frequent summer Sunday music, a sunken rose garden, a sundial, and picnic tables for the warmer weather. (If the weather's really hot and your journey home takes you south, you might want to head for Ada's Ice Cream Parlour at 118 Sydenham Road, which makes up in flavour what it lacks in decor … we can recommend the lemon meringue.) JL

ADDRESS 100 London Road, Forest Hill, London SE23 (020 8699 2339)
WEBSITE www.horniman.demon.co.uk
OPEN Monday to Saturday, 10.30–17.30; Sunday, 14.00–17.30 (the museum is likely to be closed for three months in early 2001)
GETTING THERE Forest Hill rail
BUGGIES not currently suitable for buggies (they can be left in the foyer area) WHEELCHAIR ACCESS contact the museum before visiting

Imperial War Museum

This award-winning museum is beautifully done. The approach is very much that war is about people rather than simply hardware – hence plenty of exhibits that try to offer an understanding of the nature of war. The planes, tanks, guns and so on are sensitively presented, and the building itself (once part of the Bethlem Royal Hospital, better known as Bedlam) is a pleasure to be in. Despite the tough subject matter – conflict in the twentieth century – the museum tries hard to appeal to children, with everything from Easter-egg hunts, spy-school quizzes and temporary exhibitions of the interactive, twiddly button kind, to bookable events giving 8-year-olds and up the chance to, for example, meet an actor playing the part of a First World War soldier.

On the ground floor, in a light-filled atrium space, are the large exhibits – tanks, submarines, bombers, boats and so on – with planes (including a Sopwith Camel and a Battle of Britain Spitfire) suspended as if in flight above visitors' heads. A German V2 rocket and a Polaris missile dominate the space. Alongside the fighting machines are some less-expected exhibits, such as 'Ole Bill', a London bus used on the Western Front in the First World War.

Most of this is fun even for small children. Downstairs, however, it's a bit trickier. We took our small son straight back upstairs when confronted by powerful images of emaciated refugees and injured soldiers. Many of the exhibits – such as the popular Blitz Experience in which you can feel the ground shake as bombs seem to fall around you – are not recommended for under-5s; the Belsen 1945 display is not in fact recommended for children younger than 14 unless accompanied by an adult. In short, the museum provides a thoughtful educational and emotional experience for older children, but be prepared to do a lot of explaining whatever their age. The same will no doubt go for the

museum's new wing, dedicated mostly to displays on the Holocaust, which opens in summer 2000.

There is an interesting art collection which is well worth visiting if your children will let you; it includes works by Paul Nash, Graham Sutherland, Stanley Spencer, Wyndham Lewis and Eric Ravilious among others. Above-average café serves hot food, sandwiches, salads and pastries. JL

ADDRESS Lambeth Road, London SE1 (0891 600 140 for recorded information; 020 7416 5320 for enquiries)
WEBSITE www.iwm.org.uk
OPEN daily, 10.00–18.00
COST adults £5.20, children free, concessions £4.20, disabled £2.60, concessions £1.60; free after 16.30
GETTING THERE Lambeth North Underground
BUGGIES/WHEELCHAIR ACCESS yes; improved disabled access when new wing opens summer 2000

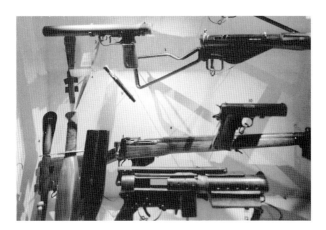

The Jewish Museum

The Jewish Museum is housed on two sites: 129–131 Albert Street in Camden Town and East End Road in Finchley. The Camden Town branch, which contains an exhibition tracing the story of the Jewish community in Britain from the Norman Conquest to recent times and an upstairs gallery that illustrates Jewish religious practice through a collection of artefacts including illuminated marriage contracts, a synagogue ark and Hanukah lamps, is interesting for adults and older children but has little to offer under-8s. The Finchley branch, however, is worth a visit.

The ground floor of this tiny museum evokes the lives of Jewish people in London at the turn of the century through recreations of a tailoring workshop – of which there were more than 1000 in Whitechapel in 1888 – a cabinet-makers' workshop and a bakery. Children can pick up the heavy irons used by the pressers – who often had one arm longer than the other as the result of lifting 16-pound weights hundreds of times a day – weigh bean bags on old-fashioned scales and see how wood joints are put together.

We didn't take our 4-year-old upstairs to the exhibition by Auschwitz survivor Leon Greenman, but it could be a good place to start to try to explain the unexplainable to older children. vw

ADDRESS 80 East End Road, London N3 (020 8349 1143)
OPEN Monday to Thursday, 10.30–17.00; Sunday, 10.30–16.30 (closed in August and on bank-holiday weekends); no café
COST adults £, OAPs £1, under-13s free
GETTING THERE Finchley Central Underground; free parking on side streets
BUGGIES/WHEELCHAIR ACCESS ground floor only

Kew Bridge Steam Museum

A little gem of a museum, housed in a nineteenth-century pumping station which supplied water to London from the 1830s until the arrival of electric technology in the 1940s, and which today is home to an impressive collection of stationary steam engines. The Boulton & Watt West Cornish, for example – so large it extends through three storeys – used to provide water for the Ealing area, while the Grand Junction engine once pumped millions of gallons per day to the Campden Hill reservoir.

At weekends and on bank-holiday Mondays these gleaming monsters are 'in steam' and this is the time to see them as they elegantly swing into action, gently hissing. You don't have to be a steam anorak to appreciate the grandeur of these machines: for children interested in machines generally, or just how things work, this is an inspiring display. Thomas-the-Tank-Engine types will be especially impressed by a ride on the miniature railway which chugs its way around the building. Operated by volunteers from the Hampshire Narrow Gauge Railway Society, it runs at special events and on some, but not all, weekends from March to November, so telephone to check it will be working before you set out. The volunteer drivers are usually happy to chat to visitors (though they were clearly deeply unimpressed by our lamentable understanding of steam engines).

The standpipe tower, the museum's dominant architectural feature, is very occasionally open (usually just twice a year) and promises – if you can manage the 261 steps – good views of the surrounding areas.

A more modern feature is the Water For Life exhibition which greets visitors on arrival: walk down a ramp alongside a wall hung with geysers, sinks, heaters, car-wash brushes and loos of varying ornateness, through a section of ring main, to a surprisingly lively exhibition all about sewers, sanitation and the supply of clean water. Children can pull drawers from a display wall (which contains a range of artefacts from Roman toilet

spoons to post-war 'Tommy Tap' posters), peep through holes to glimpse rats scurrying through pipes, or control a 'video mole', a mobile camera used to relay pictures from sewers. They can find out about the unenviable job toshers did for a living – scavenging in the sewers – and can even search with the help of a wire basket and rubber gloves through murky water for coins, silver thimbles and other 'fabulous toshroons'.

Appropriately, the museum's toilets are very spick and span (with a poster reminding us that we each flush more water down the loo in a day than someone in the third world has all week). The Babcock Café – which is open at weekends and from which you can watch the miniature railway chugging past – serves a selection of good food.

There are special events throughout the year such as the Live Steam Model Railway Show and the Historic Fire Engine Rally. The small shop sells toys, souvenirs, and some seriously trainspotterish books.

If you're making a day of it in Kew, the Royal Botanic Gardens (see page 5.22) are close by – you can catch a bus from right outside the museum. JL

ADDRESS Green Dragon Lane, Brentford, Middlesex (020 8568 4757)
OPEN daily, 11.00–17.00
COST weekends when engines are in steam: adults £3.80, children (5–15 years) £2.00, students and OAPs £2.50, family ticket £10.50; weekdays when engines are not in steam: adults £2.80, children £1.00, students and OAPs £1.50, family ticket £7.00. Children under 12 must be accompanied by an adult
GETTING THERE Kew Bridge or Gunnersbury rail; Gunnersbury Underground then bus 237 or 267; free car park
BUGGIES most parts are accessible WHEELCHAIR ACCESS partial

Livesey Museum for Children

The Livesey is so hands-on you have to spend the hour or so after a visit retraining your child to behave in the real world: 'Put that down – we're not in a museum!' It's as if the old view of museums as quiet places filled with untouchable objects and the world as a playground for noisy exploration had been reversed.

Housed in a former public library and affiliated with the Cuming Museum and South London Gallery, from whose collections it borrows, the Livesey stages new exhibitions annually, closing for a couple of months in the autumn to set up each new show. 'Mind Your Language!' (1999) covered communication and literacy with displays about the alphabet, signs and symbols, codes, Braille and advertising, and games that included talking on a walkie-talkie between a boat and a desert island. The show-stoppers of 'Number Crunching' (2000) are a 3-D snakes-and-ladders game, an interactive shop, and a casino. The exhibitions are designed to be fun, while intelligent, easy-to-read captions explain how systems we take for granted work. The dead hand of the national curriculum is nowhere to be felt, though co-curator Griff Davies says he chats informally with his daughter's teachers, while Theresa Dhaliwal hopes to set up a children's committee to give direct input.\

There's no café but you're welcome to picnic in the semi-covered court-yard. The museum runs drop-in sessions for under-5s and their carers on Thursdays from 10.00 to 12.00. VW

ADDRESS 682 Old Kent Road, London SE15 (020 7639 5604)
OPEN Tuesday to Saturday, 10.00–17.00
GETTING THERE Elephant & Castle Underground, then bus 53 or 177; free parking in side streets
BUGGIES/WHEELCHAIR ACCESS ground floor only

Museum of London

This is the place to go for a tour through 2000 years of London's past. Displays range from prehistoric settlements to the present day, taking in Roman, medieval, Tudor, Victorian and Edwardian times along the way.

Here you'll find out about everything from the pointy shoes that were all the rage in medieval times to the strange potions (such as the one made from gunpowder, oil and alcohol) taken by Londoners in an attempt to keep the great plague at bay in the seventeenth century. Children seem especially to enjoy the detailed models of, for example, Roman settlements and medieval bridges, as well as the Victorian and Edwardian tin toys and bustled dresses. (Most exhibits are displayed at a level which allows young children a good look.) Also popular is a small and rather endearing display in which Samuel Pepys' description of the Great Fire of London – which destroyed four fifths of the city in 1666 – is accompanied by a silhouetted skyline seemingly consumed by flames.

The museum's centrepiece is the eighteenth-century Lord Mayor's state coach – an explosion of red and gold ostentation. The twentieth century is represented too, by, among other things, a fabulous art deco elevator from Selfridges, a Second World War Anderson air-raid shelter, and a model of modern-day Hackney streets made up of colour photographs and transparencies.

At the centre of the museum is a garden which presents a 'living history' of London's nursery trade from the Middle Ages on. It's a surprising oasis amid all the concrete and – though more for adults than children – well worth visiting.

A good activity booklet is available from the museum shop; it's officially aimed at 7- to 11-year-olds but we found plenty in it to interest younger children too. Workshops and special family-friendly events – such as Punch and Judy shows, stone-carving demonstrations or

Museum of London

'personal appearances' by Dick Whittington – are regularly held at the museum, and it's always worth finding out about these before you visit (some require advance booking).

There is a Millburns café opposite the museum entrance serving sandwiches, hot and cold lunches, cakes, etc. Alternatively, if the weather is good, head for the nearby Barbican where the waterside restaurant offers outdoor seating by the fountains. JL

ADDRESS London Wall, London EC2
(020 7600 3699; info line 020 7600 0807)
WEBSITE www.museumoflondon.org.uk
OPEN Monday to Saturday, 10.00–17.50;
Sunday, 12.00–17.50
COST adults £5, concessions £3
(tickets valid for 12 months), under-16s
and disabled visitors free;
free admission after 16.30
GETTING THERE St Paul's Underground

National Gallery

'Utterly brilliant' is how one friend described the National Gallery children's quizzes – and they are. Aimed at young children with an accompanying adult, they generally come in the form of a booklet with questions and clues designed to send children hunting through the galleries, looking at particular paintings and responding to them in a variety of ways. The booklets are inventive and humorous, with perhaps stickers, or little flaps and doors to open in search of clues. Themed quizzes are often organised in conjunction with other children's activities during school holidays.

Ask for a copy of the current quiz at the main entrance, which is usually the starting place – it's a good idea to go armed with a pen or some crayons – and you're off. As you follow the trail around various rooms in the gallery, your children may be asked to identify pictures from small details – the claw of Uccello's dragon, for example, or a ship on the distant horizon in Claude's *Seaport with the Embarkation of the Queen of Sheba*. They are then asked to think about the painting – Has St George killed the dragon? Where is the Queen of Sheba going and what is in her luggage? – or to draw something related to it. Thus children of different ages can dip into the quizzes at whatever level suits them, whiling away a whole morning or just dropping in for half an hour.

As you move through the galleries, there are, of course, plenty of other paintings that will inevitably catch the eye. Some of them – of decapitated bodies, or St Sebastian pierced by arrows, for instance – are harder to explain than others.

The Micro Gallery, on the first floor of the Sainsbury Wing, has computer workstations which allow you (free of charge) to explore the collection by touch screen. You can look up any of the paintings from the quiz and find out more about them, or you can simply call up pictures from the gallery's collection on a subject – dragons, ships, kings or queens,

say – that particularly interests your child. There are even animation programmes so that you can, for instance, view the distorted skull from Holbein's *Ambassadors*.

If your trip to the National Gallery proves a success you might also want to try the Tate Gallery (Millbank, sw1; 020 7887 8000) where to our surprise we found it was the abstract art our children responded to best. On Sundays from 14.00 to 17.00, and on extra dates during school holidays, it runs an art trolley offering a range of activities for adults and children to do together – such as trails, games, and collages, drawings or postcards inspired by individual paintings. At the time of writing, plans for the new Tate Gallery of Modern Art (Sumner Street, se1) included a room on level 3 suggesting ways for adults and children to explore the gallery together. jl

ADDRESS Trafalgar Square, London wc2 (020 7747 2885)
WEBSITE www.nationalgallery.org.uk
OPEN daily, 10.00–18.00 (Wednesday until 21.00)
COST free (suggested donation of 50p for quiz book)
GETTING THERE Leicester Square Underground
BUGGIES/WHEELCHAIR ACCESS lifts to all floors in the Sainsbury Wing

Natural History Museum

The Natural History Museum is one of London's best attractions for children of all ages. Where else can they come face to kneebone with a towering Diplodocus skeleton, stand underneath a vast model of a blue whale, or listen to the sounds that a baby hears in the womb?

The museum is divided into two – the Life Galleries and the Earth Galleries. The latter are best approached from Exhibition Road, via a spectacular if OTT avenue of bronze statues and an elevator which whisks you up through a revolving, *Blade Runner*ish globe. Far better, we'd say, to approach the museum from the Cromwell Road entrance so that you can take in the full splendour of Alfred Waterhouse's neo-Romanesque architecture. Before you get down to the exhibits proper, take a good look at the magnificent central hall with its decorated ceiling and moulded terracotta animals, flowers and birds tucked away on columns and arches. Climb the stairs for the best view (and take a look at the giant sequoia tree on the second floor while you're at it).

The museum has a huge collection, and there is far too much to see in one visit, so it pays to have a plan of attack. One approach is to buy a 30p activity sheet from one of the shops or information desks; these are aimed at children of differing ages and cover topics such as 'Be a rock explorer' or 'Were dinosaurs like animals living today?'.

But if this is your first visit to the museum – or if your children are dinosaur-mad – then your best bet is to head for the ever-popular dinosaurs in gallery 21. Here, arranged alongside a 70-metre raised walkway, are skeletons, models and fossil remains of dinosaurs, including an impressively large Iguanodon and a scarily life-size T-rex head, plus Allosaurus, Albertosaurus and all sorts of other 'sauruses. The very young may be a little frightened of the animatronic display of meat-eaters feasting on a Tenontosaurus, but older children seem to relish it. Beneath the walkway

are touch-screen and video displays explaining more about dinosaurs. The Dinosaur Gallery's appeal remains undimmed after many visits.

Other exhibits especially popular with children in the Life Galleries are: Mammals (galleries 23 and 24), Creepy-Crawlies (gallery 33) and Human Biology (gallery 22). The Mammals Gallery, for example, includes an imposing cast of polar bears, pandas, hippos, kangaroos, elephants, and – most impressively – the suspended model of a 28-metre-long blue whale. Creepy-Crawlies is great fun (especially for the over-5s) with an enjoyably high 'yeugh' factor: here children can find out about flour mites, cat fleas, cockroaches and other bugs; they can walk through a model of an African termite mound, or discover what your average arthropod likes to eat (blood, dung balls, 'knitted niceties' …). In Human Biology, older children can get to grips with interactive displays to learn about the human mind and body. The Ecology Gallery (no. 32) is worth seeing, if only for its video wall.

In the basement of the Life Galleries, what used to be the Discovery Centre was, at the time of writing, being revamped as Investigate. The Discovery Centre was fun and this promises to be much better: a hands-on environment with plenty of specimens and IT technology for 7- to 14-year-olds (and adults) plus an outdoor space. As with the old Discovery Centre, it will be open to the public during school holidays, at weekends and late afternoons.

At the other side of the museum, in the Earth Galleries, you can find out about the planet's surface (gallery 62), take a geological tour through Britain (gallery 63) or admire jewel-like minerals (gallery 64). For most children, though, the big attraction here is the 'earthquake experience' in gallery 61 – you stand in a reconstructed Kobe supermarket as it shakes and trembles, with packets of crackers and bottles of soy sauce tumbling

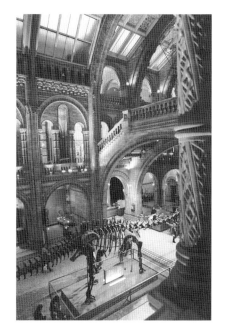

off shelves all around (though I can't help feeling it's perhaps in rather dubious taste).

Tours of the wildlife garden run during spring and summer – ask at the information desk near the main entrance for details. The garden – in the south-west corner of the grounds – has been developed to encourage many of the plants native to Britain's different landscapes. The tour is aimed more at botanically minded adults than children, but our guide took great pains to make it interesting for my son by encouraging him to look for bugs under logs, pointing out water boatmen on the pond, and so on.

Eating places include the Globe Café in the Earth Galleries, which offers kids' 'meal deals' priced at £2.75–£3.50 for a sausage/chicken nuggets/pizza-style lunch with soft drink. The Life Galleries restaurant provides hot food (chicken goujons and chips for £2.95 for instance) and children's lunchboxes for £3. There is an eating area in the basement of the Life Galleries where, during school holidays and at weekends, you can sit down to eat your own picnic lunches. Five museum shops mean that your chances of going home souvenir-less are slim. There are baby-changing facilities, and a baby-feeding room and toilets with child-level basins. JL

ADDRESS Cromwell Road, London SW7 (020 7938 9123)
WEBSITE www.nhm.ac.uk
OPEN Monday to Saturday, 10.00–17.50; Sunday, 11.00–17.50
COST adults £6.50, concessions £3.50, under-16s free; admission is free after 16.30 Monday to Friday and after 17.00 Saturday, Sunday and bank holidays. Joint season ticket for the Natural History Museum, Science Museum and V&A costs £24.00 per adult (£13.00 concessions)
GETTING THERE South Kensington Underground
BUGGIES no; baby carriers are available on loan

Pollock's Toy Museum

'Oh, we don't have a fax,' the lady at the ticket desk is explaining to someone on the telephone as we arrive. Surprising they have a telephone really, so old-fashioned is this little museum, squeezed into two adjoining houses behind Tottenham Court Road. But its olde worldiness is of course its charm. Named after Benjamin Pollock, maker of toy theatres in Hoxton in the late 1800s and early 1900s, it is crammed with everything from Victorian wax dolls, wartime teddies and magic lanterns to GI Joes, Stingrays and Sooty.

Turn right from the ticket desk through a small door which leads you up some narrow, winding stairs. Take a look as you go at the exhibits hung on the red-painted walls, such as the American money boxes, Ecuadoran bread figures or the worry beads which should be popped in a box at bedtime to ensure stress-free sleep.

This is not a hands-on museum and, with all the exhibits in glass cases, it is not really suitable for very small children or those with unguided-missile tendencies; the museum itself reckons that the ideal age is 7 to 12, though I would say a well-behaved 4-year-old would be fine. Certainly the small girl next to us was having a good time in Room 3, which contains wax dolls dressed as queens or decked out in sailor suits and bonnets.

Our favourites included, in Room 4, the 1970s dolls' house with flying ducks above the mantelpiece, pouffe and budgie cage, and the farmyard set which was made by Britain's as a 'peace toy' after the First World War and which originally included a village idiot. And, just by Room 1, the replies to correspondence from *The Boy's Own Paper* of 1882, for example: 'La Querid. Skin the bird, put on preservative and simply fill with tow. The birds can be stuffed when you get home. Refer to our "Indoor Games and Recreations".' In Room 2, children brought up on Pingu and the Teletubbies can see TV's first puppet star, Muffin the Mule.

Pollock's Toy Museum

The way out is via the museum shop which stocks a terrific selection of small, old-fashioned toys, many of them with old-fashioned prices: spinning tops, the world's smallest jigsaw, tiny things for dolls' houses, fortune-telling fish and magnetic frogs, plus toy theatres, Victorian-style scrapbooks and 'scraps'. JL

ADDRESS 1 Scala Street, London W1 (entrance in Whitfield Street) (020 7636 3452)
OPEN Monday to Saturday, 10.00–17.00, closed bank holidays
COST adults £3, under-18s £1.50
GETTING THERE Goodge Street Underground
BUGGIES/WHEELCHAIR ACCESS no

Ragged School Museum

Far from being a slice of culture imposed from above, more than any other institution we visited the Ragged School Museum involves and caters for the local community. Its story began in 1983 when a group of local residents got together to save the Victorian canalside warehouse that from 1879 until 1908 had been part of the largest ragged or free school in London, with some 1075 pupils. The museum opened in 1990 and is run by a core staff aided by some 25 dedicated volunteers, many of whom are pensioners ready to add their own and their families' recollections to the histories on show.

On permanent display is a Victorian classroom complete with brown paint, wooden desks and chairs, slates and set-your-teeth-on-edge slate pencils visitors can write with ('Imagine 80 of these in this room,' winced the presiding volunteer), a back-straightener, a barbaric device like finger-stocks for stopping children from writing with their left hands, a dunce's cap, and a cane which several of today's no-corporal-punishment pupils were queuing up to try out. Upstairs is an exhibition about growing up in the East End from the turn of the century to the present day which includes a Victorian working-class kitchen with laundry equipment and a kitchen range children can play with. On the ground floor is an exhibition called 'Tower Hamlets: a Journey through Time' which was at the planning stage as we went to press, but which curator Mary-Anne Edwards promises will have 'plenty of hands-on activities'.

During the holidays the basement is set aside for activities and exhibitions for under-7s – 'Summer at the Seaside', for instance, had a sandpit, fishing, crazy golf and postcard-making along with displays where local residents recalled seaside trips, accompanied by a soundtrack of crashing waves and seagulls. It beat a wet trip to Southend. There are also free worksheets, and workshops on Sundays and holidays: places are allo-

cated on a first-come, first-served basis on the day and topics – linked either to the permanent collection ('Meet Queen Victoria!') or to special exhibitions ('Paint a pebble') – change daily, encouraging repeat visits. The Towpath café serves drinks (good coffee) and snacks, and you're welcome to bring your own food along.

Edwards talks about consolidating facilities to meet the needs of the niche audience the museum has identified – especially under-8s – and with more than 1000 visitors over two days in one half-term holiday, it seems nearly as popular as the ragged school it once housed. VW

ADDRESS 46–50 Copperfield Road, London E3 (020 8980 6405)
OPEN Wednesday and Thursday, 10.00–17.00; first Sunday of each month, 14.00–17.00
GETTING THERE Mile End Underground
BUGGIES/WHEELCHAIR ACCESS not at present

Science Museum

Rather than have children's activities – in the form of art trolleys, activity carts or interactive information terminals – as an add-on to the main event, the Science Museum combines traditional displays with areas that allow children to get to grips with scientific concepts through experiment and exploration. The museum is so vast you could spend a day here and see less than half of it, so the following is a selective guide to the sections that are of most interest to children, starting at the bottom – and the best.

If you are with under-7s head straight for the garden in the basement. You'll pass through the Secret Life of the Home gallery, an archive of record players and wirelesses, refrigerators and hand-powered vacuum cleaners. Most memorable for children is a section of a toilet with a realistic turd in the bowl that you can watch being flushed away as you pull the chain. The garden itself looks like a trendy Barcelona bar filled with expressive works of art. There's a big steel water sculpture with pumps, dams and wheels to operate, a building zone with large-scale construction blocks, small-scale blocks on wobbly trays that simulate the effects of earthquakes without the casualties, and a bag you can load with beanbags from a wheelbarrow and hoist up two floors on a pulley before delivering the bags back to the starting point via a chute. The eyes and ears zone has a central sculpture with compartments in which you can synthesise your voice or play tunes, a booth where you can drum to piped music and shadow projectors. Allow at least an hour and prepare for a fight before you're able to leave. Things, aimed at 7- to 11-year-olds, would score highly in any other museum, though in comparison with the delights of the garden it's worldly indeed. The most interesting bits for under-8s are probably Using Things, where you can look through endoscopes to find out what's blocking pipes, experiment to see which tool works most effectively for digging up vegetables or perform a series of tests to identify

which medal is genuine, and Things and Me, where you can discover what makes a chair comfortable. There's an indoor terrace where you can picnic and a shop selling drinks and sandwiches. Look out for the large question marks on the walls which explain how the building was altered to accommodate these galleries and the function of various exposed pipes and cables.

The highlight of the ground floor is the Exploration of Space gallery, where you can peer inside the 12.9-metre-long Black Arrow R4, Britain's only satellite launch vehicle (1964–71), marvel at the scorched and battered Apollo 10 command module that took three astronauts around the moon in preparation for the 1969 landing, and see a replica of the 7-metre-high silver spider (the Apollo 11 lunar excursion module) that took two astronauts to land. There are several interactive terminals with short films and information about subjects ranging from the general (the planets) to the arcane (the German rocket arsenal). Power: The East Hall houses an impressive display of early engines, some in permanent motion including an enormous, clattering red mill engine installed to drive 1700 looms at Harle Syke Mill, Burnley, in 1903 and operational until 1970.

The Launch Pad on the first floor is like the Garden for older children without the fancy architecture. Among the 50 or so interactive exhibits are a kaleidoscope you can squeeze inside to see yourself reflected, a weighing machine, pumps that push air bubbles up a giant tube of glycerol, a turntable you can climb on, an installation with handles and pumps that enable you to move grain up tubes and along conveyor belts, and sound dishes through which you can talk to a friend at the other end of the gallery. Again there's a picnic area outside and a snack bar. Make sure you walk across the ethereal suspended glass-plank bridge, held in place by a cobweb of 372 fine stainless-steel wires and eight cables, that spans

the ground-floor gallery. Designed by Chris Wilkinson, it has sensors that react to the load on the deck and create a response in sound and light, so you can hear your own passage while your friends watch you cross on three screens opposite the Launch Pad.

After all this interaction, the near-deserted Ships galleries on the second floor seem stranded in a timewarp of glass cases and typewritten captions. Here you will find models of craft from Egyptian funerary barks (2000 BC), Greek galleys (800 BC) and Viking ships (AD 900) to the Mayflower that took the Pilgrim Fathers from Plymouth to New England in 1620, the Queen Elizabeth that made the same journey in the 1930s and the cross-channel ferry the Spirit of Free Enterprise (1980). Regrettably, it's the warships that prove the most exciting: HMS Warrior (1860), the first iron-built and armoured warship; the fearsome HMS Monarch (1911); HMS Vanguard (1944), the last battleship to be built for the British Navy. You'll also find canoes, catamarans, coracles, junks, ocean liners, racing yachts, river steamers, submarines and trawlers from around the world.

If you take the spiral staircase up to the third floor you pass a hot-air balloon which rises when you press the button that lights the burner to heat the air. The romantic Dreams of Flight gallery has a model of the beautiful Montgolfier balloon which made the first, 25-minute human flight in 1783, the Roe Triplane that flew for 300 metres in 1909, the Fokker monoplane that dominated the air war in 1915–16 thanks to an interrupter that allowed the pilot to aim his machine gun through the propeller without hitting the blades, the dragonfly-like Vimy in which John Alcock and Arthur Whitten Brown flew non-stop across the Atlantic in 1919, the fragile Gipsy Moth in which Amy Johnson flew from England to Australia in 1930, a Hawker Hurricane (1938), a Spitfire (1940), an HS125 Business Jet (1965) and an air-traffic-control suite. The Flight Lab

has interactive exhibits demonstrating how humankind achieved the seemingly impossible. Here you can sit in the cockpit of a Cessna 150, power a pedal propeller, see how a helicopter works and experiment with the effects of ailerons. It's worth popping into the Optics gallery to see the holograms and into Health Matters for the dolls'-house-scale models of a 1933 hospital and the 1998 Chelsea & Westminster.

The Glimpses of Medical History gallery on the fourth floor is for the unsqueamish only. Some 40 models including full-size reconstructions show operations ranging from eye-couching treatment for cataracts in eleventh-century Persia to open-heart surgery in 1980. Particularly gruesome is a depiction of an amputation on a ship in 1800 showing the removal (without anaesthetic) of a leg pierced by a splinter, sent to join a bucket full of previously amputated limbs beside the operating table.

At the time of writing the Wellcome Wing – a £48 million state-of-the-art 'theatre of science' housing an Imax cinema, exhibitions about contemporary issues, the human body, digital technology and the making of the modern world, and Pattern Place, a 'multisensory experience' aimed at under-8s – is under construction. The wing is billed to contain catering facilities, which is all to the good since at present the only disappointment at the Science Museum is the limited ground-floor café: as with the exhibits, it's more fun to put in the effort yourself and bring a picnic. vw

ADDRESS Exhibition Road, London SW7 (020 7938 8080)
WEBSITE www.nmsci.ac.uk
OPEN daily, 10.00–18.00
COST adults £6.50, concessions £3.50, under-16s free
GETTING THERE South Kensington Underground
BUGGY/WHEELCHAIR ACCESS yes to most galleries; plan available at desk

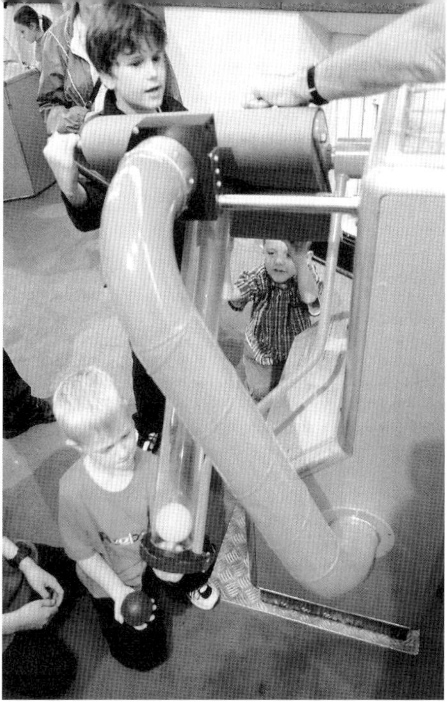

Theatre Museum

A visit to the Theatre Museum is a show in itself – though, despite its location, more amateur dramatics than West End. The imposing foyer, with its box office, red velvet curtains and two-tiered gilded boxes supported by buxom caryatids, is presided over by a flamboyantly moustachioed gentleman, then it's down the ramps – past the Wall of Fame with its handprints and signatures from famous thespians – to the exhibitions, workshops and toilets tiled with scenes from Shakespeare.

The main gallery houses an exhibition of British theatre from Shakespeare to the present – an ambitious subject staged with a lack of imagination, though we did enjoy some of the costumes and the mock dressing room. The problem perhaps stems from the fact that the museum (at the present site since 1988) was set up initially to house various bequests and collections which it has had to mould into some kind of structure. 'The Wind in the Willows from Page to Stage' exhibition, describing the creation of the Royal National Theatre's production of Kenneth Grahame's book, is also disappointingly wordy and low on visuals, though we were riveted by the video showing the actors preparing for their roles by studying the movements of real animals.

Much more successful are the workshops (free with the entrance ticket). At each of the six daily make-up demonstrations a professional make-up artist transforms a volunteer model into a restoration dame, a 1920s showgirl, a member of *Cats* (see page 8.6) or a hideously wounded victim – guaranteed to be the best face-painting you've seen. In the costume workshop volunteers are encouraged to take to the stage to model outfits that include Lady Capulet's and Sir Francis Drake's for grown-ups and child-size replicas of the gear from *The Wind in the Willows* (upper-class gent Ratty, the wide-boy weasels, their fur-coated girlfriends). The children we took loved both workshops, though I would

have appreciated more information and a bit less flourish.

The highlight of the trip was undoubtedly 'Forkbeard – Architects of Fantasy', a wonderfully interactive (and unfortunately temporary) exhibition crammed with playbills, fliers, sketches, models and peepshows. Influenced by experimental performance art of the 1960s and 1970s, Forkbeard (founded in 1974 by Tim and Chris Britton, joined in 1980 by Penny Saunders) are stage and set designers, and mount their own productions which attempt a theatre that 'accepts no rules'. Children (and adults) could operate pulleys and strings to articulate the two larger-than-life marionettes on the central stage, or make a giant rabbit at the other side of the room jump, or a Bloopy (from the show *Invasion of the Bloopies* about consumerism gone mad, featuring pink blobby creatures happy only in herds and prone to form queues behind anyone standing still) levitate (by strange coincidence, the hateful Mr Blobby appeared some six months after the show started touring …). To complement the Forkbeard show, the foyer was filled with dramatic costumes made by Mahogany Carnival Arts and others for Notting Hill including the towering, threatening Shadow of Tiananmen Square, designed in 1989 to personify the oppressive Beijing regime, and the more benign The Family, with four dolphins attached to rods that dive as the wearer moves her/his arms. Following the success of Forkbeard, exhibitions project manager Vicky Broackes assured me all future shows would be 'child-friendly and interactive' – let's hope the museum lives up to its promise. vw

ADDRESS Russell Street, London WC2 (020 7836 7891)
OPEN Tuesday to Sunday, 10.00–18.00; no café
COST adults £4.50, concessions £2.50, under-16s free
GETTING THERE Covent Garden Underground

Victoria and Albert Museum

I've always thought of the V&A as a very grown-up museum, but surprisingly its children's activities are among the best we came across. It's certainly value for money – more than 100 rooms of art, ceramics, jewellery, costume, glass, metalwork and textiles from around the world, with activities, demonstrations and performances thrown in – but unfortunately the entrance charge prohibits exploration of the collection in the most child-friendly way, through a series of short, focused visits.

The activity cart (Sundays and holidays, 10.30–17.00) is located in different galleries on different days, and offers quite sophisticated crafts exercises inspired by its setting. In the Dress Collection you can make a fan, a lace collar and cuffs, a hat or spectacles; in the Silver gallery almost every conceivable glittery material is employed to fashion goblets, plates and masks; in the Japanese gallery you can make a kimono doll or a *netsuke* and *inro* (a purse). Before you pick up your materials you are given a quiz that ensures children study in detail examples of the things they've chosen to make. Tables and chairs are provided, and if your charges are old enough you can sneak off to gaze at some of the nearby marvels.

Even better are the backpack tours, developed from an idea seen by a member of staff in Denver in the US (Saturdays and holidays, 13.30–17.00; credit card or other refundable deposit required). The Explorer takes you through the Japanese, Chinese, Islamic and Indian galleries; the Artist focuses on nineteenth-century paintings; the Antique Detective looks at various parts of the decorative-arts collection; Magic Glasses is centred on the glass collection. The key here is the props: equipped with a real rucksack and in the case of the Explorer (recommended for younger children) a pair of binoculars, youngsters find the challenges posed by the trails irresistible. Included in the Explorer pack are a jigsaw of Samurai

armour, a construction kit to replicate a Chinese bed, an egg-timer for use in a memory game and a drawing pad; as each gallery is entered the trail instructs children to find a specific object, encouraging them to look at other items in the collection. There are things to interest children in most of these galleries – Tang-dynasty statues of horses and camels; Japanese swords and armour; Tippoo's tiger, a life-sized musical automaton of an Indian tiger devouring a European – while adults can feast their eyes on sensuous statues of the Bodhisattva Guanyin or goddess Durga, slayer of the buffalo demon Mahisasura and a strong, sexy role model by contrast with the pallid Virgins and predominantly male icons of most European cultures. At weekends you're also likely to find a demonstration of anything from shoemaking to Chinese martial arts and performances that range from steel bands to Indian devotional music. And there is a selection of trails available at the information desk – tapestries, Chinese animals, Indian artefacts and so on.

Galleries you might wish to visit without the lure of special entertainment include the spectacular Plaster Casts courts, with their models of world-famous sculptures including Trajan's Column, and the Dress Collection. Most startlingly alien here are the men's clothes: late eighteenth-century dandies decked out in pedal pushers that wouldn't look amiss in French Connection; a French dress suit from the same period lavishly embroidered with flowers; a cream flannel nightgown with black tufts imitating ermine and red leather slippers worn by banker Thomas Coutts. The most extraordinary items of female attire are the English dresses from the 1740s with side hoops as wide as the skirts are long, and those in the nineteenth-century underwear cabinet which expose the structural support that underpins the seamless exteriors to shocking effect – a bit like being confronted by the services on the outside of the Centre

4.74

Pompidou. One of the pleasures is to imagine yourself in different guises: a 1860s court dress with a 2-metre embroidered train; a 1920s charleston dress with sequins, beads and gold lace; Helen Storey's 1990s biker chic in black leather and Lycra decorated with turquoise stones; Issey Miyake's rhythm-pleat box dress.

The V&A was notoriously advertised in the mid 1980s, when entrance charges were introduced, as 'an ace caff with quite a nice museum attached'. The New Restaurant does indeed serve restaurant-standard food, good sandwiches and cakes, with jazz thrown in on Sunday lunchtimes, though it's far from cheap. If you just want a snack head for the ornate Gamble Room, designed in 1868 and an example of decoration run riot. If it's fine you can picnic in the Pirelli Garden, or on wet days the Boilerhouse lunchroom is sometimes available. VW

museums and galleries

ADDRESS Exhibition Road, London SW7 (020 7938 8500)
WEBSITE www.vam.ac.uk
OPEN daily, 10.00–17.45
COST adults £5, OAPs £3.50, other concessions, under-18s and entry after 16.30 free
GETTING THERE South Kensington Underground

The Wallace Collection

It is easy to dismiss the Wallace Collection as altogether too stuffy for small children. Comprising the works of art acquired by the third and fourth Marquesses of Hertford, and the fourth Marquess' son Sir Richard Wallace, the collection is housed in an imposing building – once the family's main London residence – tucked behind Selfridges. The atmosphere as you walk into the entrance hall with its grand staircase is hushed and serious-seeming.

There are, however, very good reasons to visit the Wallace with children. Quite apart from the collection itself (old masters, French and English paintings from the early nineteenth century, miniatures, Sèvres porcelain ...) there are some excellent activities organised for 5- to 10-year-olds in the school holidays. These include workshops in which children – inspired by various paintings from the collection – create costumes from tissue paper perhaps, try out eighteenth-century French court dancing, paint their own portrait or explore the art of engraving with the help of scraper boards. They might also meet a seventeenth-century soldier and handle weapons from the Wallace's collection of arms and armour which includes some splendidly ornate pistols, swords, cannons, helmets and even models of knights astride armour-clad horses (this is easily the highlight for my 4-year-old son, worryingly fascinated by 'fighty things'). They might even join an eighteenth-century countess (actually a costumed interpreter from the Histrionix Living History Group) at the gaming tables and risk losing their inheritance in a game of cards.

Not surprisingly, the Wallace's workshops are very popular and tickets are snapped up quickly, so it's advisable to get yourself on the mailing list (020 7563 9551). During these activities, there is also an art cart for 3- to 10-year-olds which offers, for example, a monster trail or mask-making. At other times you can pick up a 50p activity sheet which takes

you on a trail of the galleries in search of paintings ('The Laughing Cavalier', for instance, or portraits of Madame de Pompadour, Queen Victoria and the Duke of Wellington). There is a shop selling postcards, books, gifts and so on.

Under the directorship of Raslind Savill the Wallace is a museum to watch. It promises to be even better by June 2000, when it will celebrate its centenary year with the opening of a courtyard designed by Rick Mather, housing a sculpture garden restaurant, four new galleries and a study centre. JL

ADDRESS Hertford House, Manchester Square, London W1 (020 7563 9500)
WEBSITE www.wallace-collection.com
OPEN Monday to Saturday, 10.00–17.00; Sunday, 14.00–17.00
COST free (donation suggested); children's workshops usually cost £2–£5; activity cart £2 per child
GETTING THERE Bond Street Underground
BUGGIES must be left at the main entrance; baby carriers are available
WHEELCHAIR ACCESS via a stairclimber only; lifts will be available when the new courtyard is completed in 2000. Telephone the access co-ordinator on 020 7563 9512

houses and gardens

Chiswick House

The oversized dolls' house that is Chiswick House, designed by the third Earl of Burlington (1694–1793) as a temple of the arts in which to display his pictures and entertain his friends (note the copious vaulted wine cellar and absence of a kitchen) is based on Palladio's Villa Capra. Highlights include the fully restored Blue Velvet Room and the lacy, elaborately coffered dome of the salon up the stone spiral staircase on the first floor.

The grounds, laid out in the 1720s by William Kent, are a popular destination for families with dogs and bicycles. You can do a pleasant circuit by walking past the regimented yew hedges, shrubberies and Ionic temple on the house side of the canal to the classic bridge, then returning along the wilder bank and across the rustic bridge beside the cascade. The grassy slope at the house side is popular for picnics; the area by the ornamental urns, sphinxes, and statues looted from Hadrian's Villa near Rome is a good play place. The café (bring your own wine) offers restaurant-standard food (Thai salmon, pasta with Roquefort sauce) as well as a children's dish, filled ciabatta and cakes. The ice cream is disappointing; we didn't sample the free dog biscuits. The semi-enclosed play space in front of the outdoor seating ensured a peaceful meal. vw

ADDRESS Burlington Lane, London w4 (020 8995 0508)
OPEN 1 April to 30 September, 10.00–18.00; 1 to 31 October, 10.00–17.00; 1 November to 31 March, Wednesday to Sunday, 10.00–16.00
COST house: adults £3.00, children £1.50, under-5s free, concessions £2.30; grounds: free
GETTING THERE Chiswick rail; Turnham Green Underground; free car park in Ellesmere Road
BUGGIES NO WHEELCHAIR ACCESS must be arranged in advance

Gunnersbury Park and Museum

This is a large, pleasant park with several hectares of grass, dramatic trees and squirrels by the dozen, good for cycling and a favourite Saturday-morning haunt for kids and dads. At the southern tip near the Potomac fishing lake the paths narrow, trees become denser and the manicured lawns give way to a more natural wooded area whose perils (thorns and nettles) and pleasures (hide and seek) children will enjoy – if you can block out the din of the traffic on the adjacent M4. The area at the back of the Large Mansion and around the Orangery provides grassy mounds, rock gardens and pleasant places to sit.

Facilities include a boating lake, pitch-and-putt golf and a well-designed playground with a separate enclosure for under-5s. The equipment for over-5s is not particularly challenging, but the absence of swings and a safety braking system on the roundabout mean parents can relax in the central gazebo or at the surrounding picnic tables. There's a small café just south of the playground and a larger pavilion-style café near the boating lake that serves pasta, jacket potatoes, burgers, sandwiches (using real bread), etc, along with lurid slush puppies, baby food and Coco Pops. The outdoor seating overlooks a small play area, so with luck you'll be able to linger in peace over your instant cappuccino or herb tea.

The park was the home of Princess Amelia (daughter of George II) at the end of the eighteenth century and of the Rothschilds at the beginning of the twentieth. The porch of the Grade II-listed Palladian Temple (c. 1750) beside the boating lake makes a fun play-stage; the Victorian Kitchens recreate a below-stairs world with occasional open days when children and staff dress up; the ugly Large Mansion (1802) houses a local-history museum. The only permanent display apart from the kitchens is a collection of state and travelling carriages; other exhibitions, all planned with children in mind, last for six months to a year. Popular items on our

trip included a 2-metre-square snakes-and-ladders board you could walk or jump on (giant dice and counters available at reception), part of a well-displayed, children-oriented exhibition on the Victorian household. Our favourites in the Treasures display, where the walls were lined with photographs and quotes from staff and frequent visitors describing their favourite museum objects, were a three-seater rocking horse and some jellies donated by Frances Brown: 'I wore these at the seaside seven years ago when I was a year old. I gave them to the museum to keep for ever and ever.' VW

ADDRESS Popes Lane, London W3 (park: 020 8993 3508; museum: 020 8992 1612)
OPEN museum: April to October, Monday to Thursday, 13.00–17.00; weekends and bank holidays, 13.00–18.00; November to March, 13.00–16.00; Victorian Kitchens: April to October, weekends and bank holidays, 13.00–18.00
GETTING THERE Acton Town Underground; free parking on side streets

houses and gardens

Ham House

As with Marble Hill House on the other side of the river (see page 5.26), the central character in the story of Ham is a woman: Elizabeth Murray, daughter of William Murray who leased the house from Charles I in 1626 but was forced into exile after the king's execution in 1649. Described by (presumably male) contemporaries as beautiful, ambitious and greedy, Elizabeth is said to have risked death by participating in the Sealed Knot, a secret organisation supporting the exiled Charles II, and to have had a liaison with Cromwell. Her second husband was the Earl of Lauderdale, and from 1677 the couple effectively ruled Scotland. After Lauderdale's death Elizabeth became a recluse, pawning pictures and jewellery to pay off her debts and fight a ruinous legal battle over her late husband's will.

The house was built in 1610, though William remodelled much of the interior in the 1630s, experimenting with new architectural styles, and Elizabeth and Lauderdale added suites of rooms along the south front in the 1670s. Children will appreciate the huge painting of the sea battle of Lepanto in the inner hall and the Great Staircase, added by William, its panels showing dragons and elephants, cannons, mortars and armour. The highlights upstairs are the North Drawing Room with its wonderfully ornate fireplace, tapestry of milkmaids and suite of dolphin chairs and the Long Gallery in which the house's inhabitants would take gentle exercise in bad weather. Among the portraits is one by Sir Peter Lely of Elizabeth with a black slave (there's a later portrait of Grace Carteret, Countess of Dysart, and a black servant holding a parrot in the Hall gallery) – rare (and shameful) representations of black Britain in this period. Downstairs I coveted the White Closet (Elizabeth's study), a small room with French doors and a beautiful walnut writing desk (just big enough for an iMac?), and the Private Closet where she entertained her friends (peep round the corner to see the incongruously erotic overmantel,

Medea Casting Spells, by William Gouw Ferguson).

Enthusiastic volunteers are at hand in the basement kitchens to explain the uses of such bizarre-looking objects as the orange spiked with cloves (to counteract human stench) and the sandals raised on metal hoops (to prevent the wearer getting the hem of her dress wet), along with more familiar whisks, bowls and pastry-cutters which children are encouraged to pick up and touch. The effect is a little like being on *Antiques Road Show*. The gardens have a Wilderness at the end furthest from the river – a geometric arrangement of tall hedges, the spaces between originally planted with wild flowers and meadow grass, representing man's control over nature – which functions as a maze for children, with four small round wooden follies to play or sit in. The Cherry Garden at the side of the house is a series of triangular and diamond-shaped beds planted with lavender and boxed by low hedges punctuated by cone-shaped topiary.

The Tearoom, with outside tables in a pleasant green area, serves hot and cold food cooked to seventeenth-century recipes including Mrs Henderson's children's lunchbox, which had a real sandwich (Mrs Henderson had charge of Elizabeth's 11 children). We also enjoyed the trail, available from the reception desk. vw

ADDRESS Ham, Surrey TW10 (020 8940 1950)
OPEN house: April to October, Monday to Wednesday and weekends, 13.00–17.00; garden: Monday to Wednesday and weekends, 11.00–18.00 or dusk
COST garden: £1.50; house: adults £5, children £2.50, under-5s free
GETTING THERE Richmond Underground, then bus 371; ferry from Twickenham (see page 5.28); free car park
BUGGIES no

Hampton Court

Begun in 1514 by Cardinal Wolsey, Hampton Court Palace was confiscated in 1529 by Henry VIII, who transformed it into one of the most modern and magnificent palaces in Europe. Further major changes were made from 1689 to 1702, when William III and Mary II employed Christopher Wren to create a royal residence to rival Versailles.

The scale is daunting, and thankfully tourists are directed along six distinct routes which can be sampled over the course of a day. There are also four separate guided tours and presentations of 20–45 minutes each by actors in costume running throughout the day. These are accessible to older children, while younger ones enjoy the many glimpses of figures in historical dress – details of these and a selection of trails are available from the information centre. The major highlights for the very young, however, are in the grounds.

The Maze, planted in 1702, is just big and dense enough to be slightly scary without any real sense of danger, and children enjoy exploring in 3-D the kind of puzzles they usually do on paper. The Wilderness which surrounds it is meadowland with long grass and wildflowers – a good place to play, with benches for adults. You can picnic here or eat in the nearby Tiltyard Tea Room, which serves sandwiches, salads, excellent cakes, hot dishes, children's lunchboxes (any five items for £2.70) and children's meals (£2.20). In the formal gardens outside the eastern entrance (in front of the Great Fountain) you can hire a horse and carriage driven by the magnificently outfitted William McWilliam and his team (£14.00 for a 20-minute trip for up to five people) to take you around the gardens and Home Park, where you'll see herons and deer.

The best part of the palace for children is the Tudor Kitchens route, which begins with a dolls'-house model of the state of play at 11.00 on Midsummer's Day in 1542 accompanied by a 10-minute commentary

giving details of the arrangements for feeding (and washing up after) a household of 1200 expecting two meals a day. The bloody butchery with its slaughtered deer and boar is followed by a series of rooms full of food and cooking equipment including areas where you can see peacock royal and marzipan desserts painted with real gold in preparation.

The 10-minute video at the start of the journey through Henry VIII's State Apartments is an accessible introduction, but nothing can prepare you for the scale of the Great Hall with its stained-glass clerestory and magnificent hammer-beam ceiling. *The Family of Henry VIII*, which shows the king with his third wife Jane Seymour and children Elizabeth, Mary and the chubby Edward, just before you enter the Royal Pew, is a good way of introducing children to the palace's former inhabitants. The pew gives an impressive view of the chapel's star-spangled Tudor ceiling.

At the start of the Wolsey Rooms and Renaissance Picture Gallery route are two small rooms lined with the linenfold panelling that for me typifies the Tudor palace. Look out for the portraits of Philip II of Spain (1527–98, one-time husband of Mary I) and his second wife Isobella in the first room – every child's fantasy of a king and queen – the Raphael self-portrait (at the age of 23) and sadly dingy Titians in the penultimate room, and Breughel the Elder's *The Massacre of the Innocents* in the last room (the children of the original were replaced in the seventeenth century by animals, so first-born boys won't lose too much sleep).

Highlights of the King's Apartments route include the spectacular staircase, the echoing Guard Chamber, its walls lined with more than 3000 pistols, muskets, bayonets and swords, the Great Bedchamber with its frieze of sphinxes and putti, and the series of red thrones culminating in the seventeenth-century toilet. In the Queen's State Apartments route look out for the grand Drawing Room with its floral decoration and camp

portrait of Queen Anne's feckless husband Prince George (1653–1708) before the fleet, and the pagoda-like blue-and-white delftware tulip vases (c. 1690) in the State Bedchamber, in which bulbs planted in each tier would send shoots through the open mouths.

The Communication Gallery in the Georgian Rooms route, with its portraits of the women at the court of Charles II (1660–85), bears out the theory that the aristocracy resemble horses. The Queen's Private Apartments, built by Wren for Queen Mary II, are the most accessible rooms for children – especially the Drawing Room, the Private Bedchamber where the king and queen slept together (there are locks on the doors and a giant silver warming-pan on the bed) and the Dining Room with its seventeenth-century Dutch paintings of sea battles.

The geometric formality of the Privy Garden held little interest for us, though the Banqueting House – built by William III in 1700 to host small after-dinner parties – with its plain, oak-panelled ante-chamber opening into an ornately and erotically painted main room with river views, is worth a visit. The near-darkness of the Lower Orangery housing Andrea Mantegna's *Triumphs of Caesar* (1484–1505) makes it hard to appreciate the paintings, though the viewing conditions mean the knights and horses stand out to almost cinematic effect. The Great Vine is the oldest known vine in the world and still produces up to 300 kilos of grapes a year. vw

ADDRESS Hampton Court Road, East Molesey, Surrey (020 8781 9500)
OPEN March to October, 9.30–18.00; November to February, 9.30–16.30
COST palace and grounds: adults £10, concessions £7.60, over-5s £6.60; grounds (not including Maze): free; Maze: adults £2.10, concessions £1.30; Privy Gardens: adults £2.10, concessions £1.30
GETTING THERE Hampton Court rail; car park £3

Highgate Cemetery and Lauderdale House

Nancy: 'Does the big graves mean people loved them more?'

Looked at from Nancy's perspective, Highgate Cemetery offers countless opportunities for socio-economic observation, as well as a chance to deal with those difficult questions about death and dead bodies, and an exciting wild playspace that makes a pleasant change from the predictability of parks and playgrounds.

One of the biggest of the graves in Highgate's Eastern Cemetery, of course, belongs to Karl Marx (1818–83: 'The philosophers have only interpreted the world in various ways. The point however is to change it'), whose monumental grey marble monolith topped by an enormous bust stands next door to the much more modest tribute to Claudia Jones (1915–64), founder of the Notting Hill Carnival and 'valiant fighter against racism and imperialism who dedicated her life to the progress of socialism and the liberation of her own black people'. Make of the difference what you will. Nineteenth-century family tombs provide sobering reading: William Fogg and Amelia Papprill lost their two middle children aged 3 in 1869 and 1871; their eldest drowned at the age of 14; their youngest died aged 17. And economics is also apparent in the contrast between the grandiose marble slabs of the family tombs near the entrance and homemade monuments such as the wooden cross with stuck-on lettering that marks the grave of Steven Spilling, who died in 1990 aged 17 months.

Once you stray off the paved paths you find yourself in a fantastic jungle littered with ivy-encrusted gravestones that look like deformed tree stumps and criss-crossed by tracks you have to fight your way along. Other famous inhabitants include Mary Anne Evans (George Eliot,

1819–80), commemorated by a simple obelisk to the right of the last path on the left before Marx's overweening memorial, and Australian painter Sidney Nolan (1917–92), whose simple square stone slab can be reached by scrambling determinedly through the ivy to the right of the turning before this (squashed in front of him lies print journalist and lesbian artist Catherine Arthur (1937–91), whose Cancer Drawings remain one of my own favourite odes to mortality).

Next door is Waterlow Park, a pleasant green area sprawling down the hill with a tiny playground at the bottom and a large pond in the middle. Lauderdale House, in the north-eastern corner, holds exhibitions and fairs as well as drop-in children's shows on Saturday mornings at 10.00 and 11.30 and under-3s music (see page 7.14) on Mondays at 12.00. The café serves an unusual variety of dishes (house specialities include baked avocado stuffed with rice and mushrooms, liver and bacon, and crêpes) as well as a standard children's menu and uninspiring cakes. Beware: as the tacky wedding photographs and grovelling thank-you notes at the entrance imply, you may be invaded by drunken revellers on Saturday afternoons. vw

ADDRESS Swain's Lane, London N6 (020 8340 1834)
OPEN Western Cemetery: by guided tour only; Eastern Cemetery: April to October, 10.00–17.00; November to March, 10.00–16.00
COST £1
GETTING THERE Archway Underground; free parking on side streets

Royal Botanic Gardens, Kew

Despite its role as a laboratory for plant conservation and generation, you can wander almost freely around Kew Gardens' 120 hectares of manicured lawns and orchestrated planting juxtaposed with areas left pleasingly wild. If you want to avoid the crowds, head through the Woodland Glade to the west towards the river. Otherwise, the area within easy reach of Victoria Gate on Kew Road offers a good mix of things to see and places to hang out and picnic in – we particularly recommend the lawns dotted with low-branched spreading cedars between the Palm House and Temperate House with their views of William Chambers' clunky pagoda.

Decimus Burton's ethereally transparent, sculpturally dramatic Palm House (1844–48) is as awe-inspiring inside as out. Our children loved doing raindances under the periodic showers that maintain the humidity and enjoyed the view from the 10-metre-high gallery. The highlight of the poorly captioned Marine Display in the basement was some waving brown kelp that allegedly grows 45 centimetres a day to a length of 100 metres. Burton's more ornate Temperate House (1860–69) is less exciting, though it's worth passing through on the way to the seething volcano in the ugly Evolution House nearby. A short walk in the opposite direction takes you to the Marianne North Gallery – a room lined with 832 oil paintings of flowers and plants from Australia, Borneo, Brazil, Canada, Japan and South Africa that this remarkable Victorian painted on her travels. The paintings are inset in panelling made from 246 types of wood she collected, and the gallery was designed under her supervision.

The Princess Diana Conservatory (1986) on the other side of the Palm House is surprisingly functional and rectilinear, though the coy way it peeps out from the protective, fun-to-play-on mounds that surround it and the constantly shifting louvred blinds that shade its contents did remind me of those lowered eyes and flick-fringe screen. Paolozzi's bronze

at the Palm House end is a no-go area for children; walk to the other side to explore the brick paving dotted with naked footprints – artist Reinhild Beuther's *Not Quite Knowing*. Inside, the Moist Tropics zone has lush greenery, pools of koi and a central aquarium of freshwater fish from Africa and South America, as far as we could tell from the inadequate captioning. The Dry Tropics zone is devoted to cacti – phallic, pumpkins, snakes, faces … The Orchid Zone is straightforwardly gorgeous, whether the muted whites and lilacs of the tropical flowers or the more gaudy temperate varieties. The densely displayed 'Plants + People' exhibition in the Museum beside the lake has an impressive touch-screen display of information and pictures of some 70,000 objects from Kew's collection. There are also touch-screen quizzes and boxes where you can explore sounds and smells – along with facts about how we use plants (did you know that Concorde's engines rely on coconut oil?).

If you're not picnicking, the best place to eat is the Pavilion Restaurant on the far side of the Marianne North Gallery, which has lots of outdoor seating and specialises in stir-fries and bakes, salads, sandwiches and cakes (children's lunchboxes £2.50 for five items). The Orangery, a pleasant lofty space, serves hot food and salads with no concessions to children; the Bakery does pizza, jacket potatoes and ice cream. Be warned: at the Victoria Gate café a ham sandwich costs £4.25. VW

ADDRESS Kew Road, Richmond, Surrey TW9 (020 8332 5655)
OPEN daily, from 9.30 to between 16.00 and 19.30 depending on season; glasshouses close at between 15.45 and 17.30
COST adults £5, children £2.50, under-5s free, family ticket £13.00
GETTING THERE Kew Gardens rail/Underground; car park £2 in summer, free in winter

Marble Hill House and Twickenham Riverside

Marble Hill House is a delightful Palladian villa built in 1724–29 for Lady Henrietta Howard, mistress of George II. It's worth catching the 10-minute video, which pays tribute to the intelligence and determination that enabled this remarkable woman to build a house of her own, and pausing to admire the great mahogany staircase, made of trees from Honduras. The impressively carved and gilded Great Room on the first floor contains Roman landscapes probably painted for the house by Giovanni Paolo Panini in 1738 as well as portraits of Queen Henrietta Maria with a dwarf and a monkey and Charles I with a young Prince Charles decked out in a floor-length green-velvet dress, both after Van Dyck (c. 1633). The second-floor rooms have some extraordinary pictures and furniture including a series of Chinese paintings of birds and scenes on mirrors and black paper.

The sparsely planted park is largely devoted to sports grounds (a one o'clock club beside the car park and an over-5s adventure playground with a registering system are aimed at locals); the grassy slope on the river side of the house is a tranquil place to picnic. Otherwise, the ivy-covered Coach House café has a good breakfast menu and limited lunch menu – the children's Marble Hill Platter (raisins, crisps, and slices of apple, carrot and cheese) was universally appreciated and the service was the most child-friendly I've come across. Or you could walk west along River-side to the White Swan, with a terrace by the river opposite Eel Pie Island.

Orleans House can be reached via a gate on Orleans Road. All that remains is a charmingly baroque octagonal pavilion with wings, designed by James Gibbs in 1720 to receive Caroline, the future wife of George II. It's now a gallery and runs activity sessions at weekends and holidays. On the other side of Riverside is a small playground. Here you can get

Marble Hill House and Twickenham Riverside

the Hammertons ferry (weekends, 10.00–18.30 or dusk; weekdays February to October, 10.00–18.00; adults 40p, children 20p) to Ham House (see page 5.8) or hire a rowing boat to explore the river.

The gardens of York House, built c. 1635 by Scottish courtier Andrew Pitcarne and now council offices, are also worth a visit. Immediately in front of the house is the York House Canteen café (open Monday to Friday, 7.30–17.00), a vast sunken lawn with steeply sloping sides ideal for rolling down and a very pretty Japanese garden, but the highlight is a fountain acquired by Sir Ratan and Lady Tata, in 1906 – cross the steeply arched bridge over Riverside and follow the sound of running water. Here seven life-size naked sea-nymphs posed like showgirls on rocks or shells pay homage to a goddess atop two rearing horses. Presumably intended to approximate the effect of Rome's Trevi fountain, it has become overgrown with pondweed and ivy to surreal effect. vw

ADDRESS Richmond Road, Twickenham (Marble Hill House: 020 8892 5115; Orleans House: 020 8892 0221)
OPEN Marble Hill House: April to September, 10.00–18.00; October, 10.00–17.00; November to March, Wednesday to Sunday, 10.00–16.00; Orleans House: April to September, Tuesday to Saturday, 13.00–17.30, Sunday, 14.00–17.30; October to March, Tuesday to Saturday, 13.00–16.30, Sunday, 14.00–16.30
COST Marble Hill House: adults £3.00, concessions £2.30, children £1.50, under-5s free; Orleans House: free; York House gardens: free
GETTING THERE St Margarets or Twickenham rail/Richmond Underground then buses 33, 290, 490, H22, R68, R70; free car park
BUGGIES/WHEELCHAIR ACCESS Marble Hill House: no buggies, wheelchairs ground floor only

Syon Park

The twelfth Duke of Northumberland has exploited the crowd-pulling potential of his London home to the full and beyond, with the result that this is a fun, if expensive, day out.

The lakeside grounds, laid out by 'Capability' Brown in the mid eighteenth century, rank for my money with Isabella Plantation (see page 1.36) as the most beautiful stretch of garden in London. Ignore the Lakeside Walk through the Duke's private woodland, a muddy path with a fence on one side and the lake on the other, and instead explore the far bank, where several meandering routes cut through a collection of exotic shrubs and trees ranging from the spindly Pond Cypress (the tallest recorded tree in Britain) to the near-horizontal Indian Bean Tree dipping its branches into the water. Look out for turtles sunning themselves on the ramps. At the far end is Flora's Lawn, a big green space dominated by a doric column supporting a statue of Flora, goddess of flowers. Cross the hump-backed bridge and you're in a meadow that makes a perfect picnic spot. For £1 (children 50p) return at weekends from April to October you can make the trip courtesy of the Coronation, a miniature steam engine.

The ethereal Great Conservatory with its bulbous central dome, designed in 1820 by Charles Fowler, the architect of Covent Garden market, has cacti at one end (we liked the one with a face punched through its leaves) and a grotto with running water and goldfish at the other. Walk through the formal gardens, where the peacocks strut their stuff, past the fish pond dominated by a statue of Mercury to the ice house, a semi-underground chamber built to store barrow-loads of ice hacked from the lake in winter to use in summer to cool drinks and sorbets.

The castle-like Syon House, built in the mid sixteenth century with interiors remodelled by Robert Adam in the 1760s, has little for children. The imposing and relatively austere monochrome Great Hall gives

way to a blue-and-gold Ante-Room with gilded nude statues at gallery level and a magnificent patterned floor, the Red Drawing Room, its sidetables topped by mosaics looted from the Baths of Titus in Rome, and the mauve, green and gold Long Gallery, 'finished in a way to afford variety and amusement' to the ladies of the house. At the end of the Oak Passage lined with royal and family portraits is the almost cinematic *Belshazzar's Feast*, a painting on glass by visionary nineteenth-century artist John Martin.

Without paying to go into the house or grounds you can eat at the Patio Restaurant, which serves salads, sandwiches, cakes and a choice of four hot meals (children's portions £3.50; children's meals £3.95), and visit several other attractions. The beating wings and low-flying objects in the London Butterfly House – a large, plant-filled conservatory with fish ponds spanned by bridges – are disconcerting at first, but soon the enchantment of watching some 30 species, displaying an extraordinary variety of colours and markings, feed, nest and rest kicks in. Look out for the three emerging cages where chrysalises specially bred in Thailand and Costa Rica hang on sticks, and the ants' feeding table where you can watch the eternal workers, laden with food, struggle across a rope. On the way out is an exhibition of the kind of things little boys are supposed to be made of, as well as tarantulas, scorpions, silkmoths and millipedes, and a shop selling items of dubious relevance.

The Aquatic Experience has a pool of satiny koi, bred for the beauty of their markings, which you can reach in and touch, as well as a pen of huge African leopard tortoises with shells like inside-out coffered ceilings that children can stroke. We liked the red-eared terrapin, the giant gourami and the sucker-mouthed catfish; the crocodile was hiding but the Burmese python was scary enough. Though billed as an educational

and conservation project, its shop too seemed highly commercial. Both attractions have small gardens where you can picnic for free.

If you need a rest but your children are still going, take them to Snakes and Ladders, an indoor adventure playground along the lines of Bramley's Big Adventure (see page 7.6). The glazed roof and cheerful decor mean the café, which sells burgers, jacket potatoes, sandwiches and babyfood, is relatively pleasant and you can borrow magazines for a £2 deposit. There is also a sizeable outdoor seating area next to a deserted playground whose climbing equipment can't compete with the jungle within.

Syon also has a garden centre, farm shop, tropical and marine fish shop, trout fishery, needlecraft shop, pet shop and hydroponic-systems shop. vw

ADDRESS Brentford, Middlesex TW8 (020 8560 0881)
OPEN gardens: 10.00–17.30; house: April to October, Wednesday, Thursday, Sunday, 11.00–17.00; Butterfly House: 10.00–17.00 summer; 10.00–15.30 winter; Aquatic Experience: April to September, 10.00–18.00; October to March, 10.00–17.00; Snakes and Ladders: 10.00–18.00
COST gardens: adults £3.00, children over 4 and concessions £2.00, family ticket £14.00; house and gardens: £5.80/£4.00/£6.00; Butterfly House: adults £3.30; children over 2 and concessions £2.00; family ticket £7.75; Aquatic Experience: £3.00/£2.50/£10.00; Snakes and Ladders: £2.25–£4.65 for two hours depending on age of child and time
GETTING THERE Gunnersbury Underground then bus 237 or 267 to Brentlea Gate bus stop; free car park
WHEELCHAIR ACCESS House: no

landmarks

London Eye

Like Harry Lime in *The Third Man*, you can now hang from a giant wheel overlooking the city's uncertain limits (and in this case the terraces of the Houses of Parliament) and wonder, 'Would you really worry if one of those dots stopped moving?' When will they open the sewers?

London's millennial wheel is not in fact a Ferris wheel: the 135-metre-high network of spokes, dwarfed only by Canary Wharf, the Telecom tower and the NatWest tower, is hung on a single A-frame, not two. Designed by Julia Barfield and David Marks, its hallmark is transparency, both for the bicycle-wheel-like frame and the 32 egg-shaped glass capsules, each capable of accommodating up to 25 people, that allow all-round visibility (even downwards). Though the wheel was not operational at the time of writing, passengers will be allowed to walk around and the structure will move so slowly it won't need to stop to let you on and off. The enterprise has something of the streamlined feel sponsor British Airways would no doubt like to achieve in its own services.

Unlike New York or Paris, London has no other such public viewing platform, and whether the wheel's popularity will engender a campaign to extend its five years of planning permission remains to be seen. I'd certainly vote for the pleasure to be had from unexpected glimpses of the skeletal structure around town. Like the Dome (see page 6.4), its status as fairground ride or public monument is uncertain – and as we enter a new millennium, it does seem extraordinary that big is still beautiful. vw

ADDRESS Jubilee Gardens, Belvedere Road, London SE1 (020 7654 0800)
OPEN April to October, 9.00–22.00; November to March, 10.00–18.00
COST adults £7.45, children £4.95, for a 30-minute ride
GETTING THERE Waterloo Underground and rail
BUGGIES no; baby-carriers available

Millennium Dome

Press times for this guide meant that we had only a preview visit to the Richard Rogers-designed Dome before its controversial opening in January 2000. The first thing our 4-year-old noted (approvingly) was that as you approach 'it smells of chips'. Not surprising, since McDonald's is a sponsor and major presence, with outlets inside (between masts 9 and 10) and outside (near the entrance). And some hours later – tired, hungry and domed-out – we were pitifully grateful for a sit-down and a Happy Meal. Because 'doing' the dome is a demanding business.

There are 15 zones and you should plan to spend the whole day here if you want to visit more than a few. There is disappointingly little for young children, though an undoubted hit is Timekeepers of the Millennium – a three-storey *Blade-Runner*-meets-Heath-Robinson tower in which kids shoot at other visitors with foam balls. That seemed to be the idea, anyway. Our son would happily have stayed there all day. The Play Zone meanwhile offers interactive fun – such as a tug of war with an on-screen figure – but small children will not have the patience to queue for their turn (and older children probably have something more exciting on their computer at home). Other zones had their moments – oversized table football in the Work Zone, slot machines in the otherwise daft Living Island. The Nigel Coates-designed Body Zone in which you can take a Numbskull-style trip through the human body (not completed when we visited) looked pink and orange and fabulous on the outside at least, and the British Spaceways ride in Home Planet seemed promising. The serene James Turrell room in the Eva Jiricna-designed Faith Zone was, for me, the real highlight, but when you're 4 'it's boring'.

At the time of writing the 'Millennium Show' was taking a critical drubbing; I'm embarrassed to say I found the aerial acrobatics dazzling. As the artists spin way above your head you have, for the first time, a

sense of the sheer size of the place. (As you enter the dome you are given a timed ticket for this show and for the *Blackadder Back and Forth* film which is shown in the Skyscape cinema, outside the main building.)

Getting to the Dome on the Jubilee line was much easier than we'd expected. We were pleased that we'd visited what is now one of London's most famous landmarks. But ultimately it has the feel of a trade show gone mad rather than a millennial vision. And £57 for a family ticket? I couldn't help thinking we would have had a better time at Legoland. JL

ADDRESS North Greenwich, London SE10 (0870 606 2000)
WEBSITE www.dome2000.co.uk
OPEN 10.00–18.00 plus some evenings
COST adults £20.00, children £16.50, under-5s free, family ticket £57.00
(up to five people). Entry by advance booking only
GETTING THERE North Greenwich Underground (the area around the
Dome is billed as a 'no-car zone')

St Paul's Cathedral

St Paul's Cathedral, the architectural masterpiece of Christopher Wren, is one of London's greatest landmarks and an active place of Christian worship. It's also the last resting place of, among others, the Duke of Wellington, Horatio Nelson and Florence Nightingale.

But for children, of course, its real appeal is its dome – particularly the Whispering Gallery, 259 steps up, where you really can whisper into the wall and be heard by someone on the other side. Pause here to fail miserably to instil in your children an appreciation of the architectural and spiritual magnificence that surrounds them before climbing another 119 steps (steeper ones, this time) to the Stone Galleries. From here, on a clear day, you'll have breathtaking views all over London (it's worth taking a pair of binoculars). There is another gallery – the Golden Gallery – which is 85 metres and 530 steps up, but I wouldn't recommend it unless you and your children are fit, agile and not at all bothered by heights or winding staircases. I really wouldn't try it with very young children.

The 'Explorer's Guide', available from the shop near the cathedral entrance, includes puzzles and odd snippets such as the fact that Nelson's body was preserved in a barrel of brandy before being buried here … JL

ADDRESS St Paul's Churchyard, London EC4 (020 7236 4128)
OPEN Monday to Saturday from 8.30, galleries from 9.30 (last admission 16.00). Cathedral occasionally closed for services
COST prices are for entry to cathedral, with additional cost of admission to galleries given in brackets. Adults £4 (+ £3.50), children aged 6–16 £2 (+ £1.50), under-6s free, family ticket for two adults and two children £9 plus £1 for each additional child (+ £7.50), concessions £3.50 (+ £3)
GETTING THERE St Paul's Underground
BUGGIES/WHEELCHAIR ACCESS to cathedral floor and crypt only

Tower Bridge Experience

Don't be too put off by the naff addition of the word 'Experience' – nor by the ticket queue which, at holiday times, moves at an agonisingly slow pace. This is a chance to get inside one of London's most famous landmarks. You enter via the north tower and ascend by lift as far as level two. From here you are guided along a series of multimedia presentations which, leading up to the high-level walkways and then down the south tower, tell the history of the bridge and how its daring design solved the problem of providing a crossing point over what was the busiest stretch of river in the world – without interfering with shipping.

Along the way you'll meet the animatronic Harry Stoner, who explains why the bridge was so badly needed, and gives an idea of what it was like to be one of the 432 construction workers toiling on this masterpiece of Victorian engineering, the most sophisticated bascule bridge ever built. It was begun in 1886 and completed eight years later, when cheering crowds gathered to watch the Prince and Princess of Wales give 'the Wonder Bridge' its official opening. Also part of the tour is a mock bascule chamber with a film explaining the hydraulic system which originally lifted the bridge.

You should allow about an hour and a half for the tour, which involves trekking up quite a few stairs (if you can't manage them there are lifts). As you go, glance down through the girders to glimpse the traffic passing below. Many of the presentations aren't really aimed at young children, however, so you might want to skip some of them and head straight for the glazed high-level walkways, which as far as we're concerned are by far the best bit. Once intended for pedestrian traffic across the Thames, these offer terrific views west towards the Telecom Tower and St Paul's, and east towards Canary Wharf and the Millennium Dome. Little windows can be opened for taking pictures, or preferably for poking your

nose out on windy days when it is sometimes so blustery it makes your hair stand on end.

Finish your trip with a visit to the engine room and the Hands-On Gallery, where children can operate a variety of interactive models of the bridge or its hydraulic machinery. During school holidays, children's activities such as kite-making are often arranged.

If you possibly can, plan your visit to Tower Bridge to coincide with an opening (you can find out about opening times by ringing 020 7378 7700). Alternatively ask one of the guides at the Tower Bridge Experience when the next bridge lift will be. We happened to be there when HMS Belfast (see page 3.6) was towed through on her way to dry dock in Portsmouth, and it was a fantastic sight. JL

ADDRESS Tower Bridge, London SE1 (020 7378 1928)
WEBSITE www.towerbridge.org.uk
OPEN daily (closed for maintenance one day each year), April to October, 10.00–18.30, November to March 9.30–18.00 (last admission an hour and a quarter before closing)
COST adults £6.15, students and OAPs £4.15, children 5–15 £4.15, under-5s free, family ticket (two adults and two children) £15.50
GETTING THERE London Bridge, Fenchurch Street rail; Tower Hill Underground; Tower Gateway DLR

Tower of London

First the downside. The Tower is one of London's biggest tourist attractions and is nearly always heaving with school groups, tourists and tour guides brandishing brollies. Tickets aren't cheap and you'll probably have to queue for them. Another point to remember is that the place is full of steps and winding stone staircases rather than lifts (parts of the Tower were built more than 900 years ago, after all) and is therefore not an ideal destination for those with very small children, buggies or wheelchairs.

On the upside, however, the Tower of London is full of things to excite young imaginations and – because it has both gore and glamour – seems to appeal to boys and girls alike.

The grisly bits first. As well as the scaffold site on which Anne Boleyn, Lady Jane Grey and others lost their heads, the Traitors' Gate through which many prisoners made their final journey, and the Bloody Tower in which legend has it the little princes, the sons of Edward IV, were murdered, there is the rather spectacular royal armouries collection in the White Tower. Here you'll see swords, some very impressive royal armour, columns of pikes and pistols, a 'heading axe' and execution block. You are asked to leave all buggies at the entrance, and warned that the complete tour takes at least 45 minutes and involves 200 steps (though for softies there is a 20-minute route involving 50 steps).

Dating back to the eleventh century, the White Tower is the most imposing building here – what's generally thought of as the Tower. By the 1600s it contained the largest store of gunpowder anywhere in England – lucky, then, that the Great Fire stopped just short of here in 1666. The way out leads you to one of the Tower of London's four shops where you can buy, say, a model block and axe or, should the fancy take you, a fibreglass replica of Henry VIII's foot combat armour.

You may feel at this point that it's time for a bit of glitz, in which case

head for Waterloo Barracks where the Crown Jewels are kept. Videos and regal music keep you semi-entertained as you line up to get a look at them. And quite a quick look it is too, because you are whisked past on a travelator (small children will need to be lifted up to get a good view). Fabulously ostentatious orbs, sceptres and crowns parade by, dazzlingly set with vast diamonds, chunks of rubies, and huge sapphires and pearls. Showiest among the Crown Jewels are the Sceptre with the Cross set with the pebble-sized Cullinan 1 diamond, and the Imperial State Crown with its 2868 diamonds, 17 sapphires, 11 emeralds, five rubies and 273 pearls. The dainty diamond mini-crown was made for Queen Victoria who insisted, sensible woman, that wearing a heavy crown gave her a headache.

There is a fashion statement of a different kind to be found in the unique uniforms worn by the Yeoman Warders ('Beefeaters') who live at the Tower with their families – you can sometimes spot their washing hanging out to dry. The Tower's other famous residents are of course the ravens, which seem to fascinate some young visitors – perhaps because of the macabre fact that they used to feast on the remains of executed prisoners, or perhaps because of the legend that says the kingdom will fall if they leave. Don't get too close though, because they can bite. One of the Yeoman Warders – the Ravenmaster – takes care of the eight ravens who currently live inside the Tower walls. Each has its own name, territory and colour-coded tag – they even have their own gravesite.

Worth seeing if you have the time/energy is the Medieval Palace, where costumed guides explain what life was like when monarchs lived here.

During school holidays special events are sometimes arranged for children – a leaflet available from the information kiosk near the main entrance gives details. Alternatively you can buy the rather good children's activity booklet, priced £1.99.

There is a food kiosk near the Ravens' Lodgings, and two Pret à Manger outlets outside on the wharf (ask for a re-entry permit if you want to return to the Tower). You can also sit and picnic on benches while enjoying views of Tower Bridge and the Thames. Snack kiosks of varying quality stand near the main entrance, plus a 280-seater McDonald's complete with shop. Alternatively wander east along the wharf to St Katharine's Dock, a surprisingly pleasant place given how ugly the next-door Tower Hotel is. Here you can find a family-friendly meal at Pizza on the Dock at the Dickens Inn (020 7488 2208) and admire yachts and larger vessels such as the Grand Turk, a replica of an eighteenth-century man o' war used in the filming of the TV drama, *Hornblower*. JL

ADDRESS Tower Hill, London EC3 (020 7709 0765; recorded information 020 7680 9004)
WEBSITE www.hrp.org.uk
OPEN March to October, Monday to Saturday, 9.00–17.00, Sunday 10.00–17.00; November to February, Tuesday to Saturday, 9.00–16.00, Sunday and Monday, 10.00–16.00 (buildings inside close half an hour after last admission time)
COST adults £11.00, children 5–15 £7.30, under-5s free, family ticket (five people including up to two adults) £33, concessions £8.30
GETTING THERE Tower Hill Underground; Tower Gateway DLR; Fenchurch Street, London Bridge rail; riverboat from Charing Cross, Westminster or Greenwich
BUGGY/WHEELCHAIR ACCESS limited; a number of wheelchairs are available for free hire from the Group Ticket Office

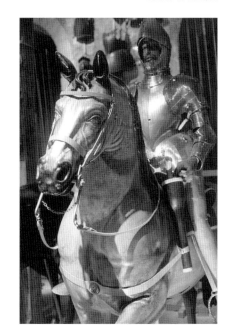

hands-on

Art 4 Fun: The Creative Café

The idea of Art 4 Fun (and presumably the spelling) came from California. Ria Berger: 'One plate and I was hooked! After I'd finished my second dinner service, David and I realised we had to introduce the concept to the UK.' It's marketed as an alternative to the traditional 'hen night', stress-management-course venue or office-workers' lunchtime routine. As a place to hang out with children it has much to recommend it.

The café aspect is taken lightly: on our lunchtime visit there were no sandwiches available and people were bringing in anything from picnics to pizzas. But the bring-your-own policy enables you to concentrate effort and financial resources on the art at hand, while going out in search of sustenance represents a welcome break from watching the paint dry. You can decorate greetings cards, T-shirts, glasses, mugs, plates, tiles, picture frames, cardboard boxes and a variety of hideous garden-teddy-bear-type objects. You decide what you want to tackle, tell one of the helpful staff, then collect whatever paints and brushes you need and get going. If you have younger children, I'd recommend a cardboard box as these are unbreakable, cheaper, use quicker-drying acrylic paint with a wider range of colours and can be taken away rather than having to collect them after they're fired. We spent two and a half hours there, and no one objected to all the colour-mixing experiments, changes of mind, or mess. VW

ADDRESS 444 Chiswick High Road, London W4 (020 8994 4100)/212 Fortis Green Road, London N10 (020 8444 4333)/172 West End Lane, London NW6 (020 7794 0800)
OPEN Monday to Saturday, 10.00–22.00; Sunday and holidays 10.00–20.00
COST £3 for unlimited use of materials; objects are £2.75 upwards
GETTING THERE Chiswick Park Underground/West Hampstead Underground

Baby Massage

Unless you're a naturist or a sauna aficionado, it's not often you get the chance to sit in a room with ten naked people. And the great thing about naked babies is they don't mind if you stare. Sure enough, as with adults, they come in many shapes and sizes beyond the chubby stereotype advertising has brainwashed us into believing is the norm: long legs or long backs, skinny limbs or folds of flesh, narrow shoulders, pear-shaped.

Baby massage, for pre-crawlers, encourages babies to explore space after the confinement of the womb and can improve circulation and digestion – it's a bit like a first work-out, and they often reward you afterwards with long, deep sleep. Arlene Dunkley-Wood begins her classes with relaxation exercises for the adults ('babies are a barometer of your moods, and there's no point in starting if you're not relaxed too') before the first contact: firm downward strokes from shoulders to toes. Other exercises involve stretching the arms and legs, massaging wrists, fingers, ankles and feet, squeezing the colon to ease wind, stroking the back and 'bicycling'. Parents are encouraged to enjoy their babies' bodies and to handle them confidently; babies (as long as they don't mind being undressed) love the sensations and the undivided attention. Afterwards there's fruit tea and biscuits and a chance to compare notes – almost inevitably about sleep.

Yogahome also runs Yogabugs for 4- to 11-year-olds (see page 7.24) and postnatal yoga. Bring your own towel; mats, rugs and sweet almond oil are provided; dress lightly as the room is very warm. VW

ADDRESS 11 Allen Road, London N16 (020 7249 2425)
OPEN Thursday, 10.00–11.30
COST £7.50; numbers restricted so advance booking advisable
GETTING THERE buses to Newington Green; free street parking

Bramley's Big Adventure

If it's a couple of hours of uninterrupted time you're after, indoor activity playgrounds have one great advantage: no matter how demanding your offspring, you can't follow them into the three-storey maze of nets, slides and ball pools such places offer. On the downside, many indoor activity playgrounds provide an environment for carers no one would seek out. Bramley's is an exception, with a light, airy café serving decent food (jacket potatoes, nuggets, pasta, good coffee), free magazines (many past their sell-by date, but better than a doctor's surgery) and attitude.

The brochure's boasts of balance beams, an aerial runway, a roller squeeze, monkey swings and a spooky den were impossible to verify, though I did see for myself the wavy and spiral slides and got good reports of the wobbly mirrors. There's also a separate area for under-5s (restrictions on younger children entering the over-5s area are not enforced) and a small space with soft cushions for babies. In termtime the centre runs additional free activities (colouring, music, messy play, dressing-up clothes) for under-5s from 10.00 to 13.00 and there are holiday workshops for older children.

As for the attitude, 'Bramley's supports a mother's right to feed her child by whatever method she chooses', refuses to stock Nestlé products and has information about the campaign against Nestlé's supply of infant formula to developing countries in reception. vw

ADDRESS 139 Bramley Road, London W10 (020 8960 1515)
OPEN daily, 10.00–18.30
COST for 90 minutes: over-5s schooldays £3.75, weekends and holidays £4.25; under-5s £2.75/£3.25
GETTING THERE Ladbroke Grove Underground; parking £1 in Westway Sports Centre opposite

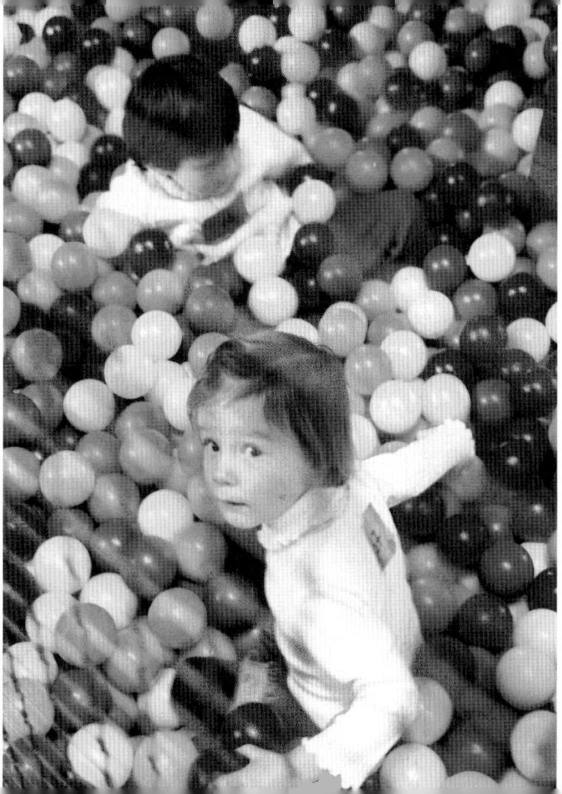

Cyberia

Surfing the web in one of London's increasingly ubiquitous cybercafés isn't the cheapest way to do it, but if you haven't got access at home and your local library isn't wired up yet, it's a pleasant way to pass an hour or so. We chose Cyberia not because it offers anything special for children, though staff are friendly and helpful, but because it was the first such café to be established, the food and coffee are good, and it's in central London.

Time is money in cyberspace, so consult Ask Jeeves (www.ajkids.com) which works as an efficient search engine and an encyclopaedia for older children, though it doesn't quite live up to its promise of answering 'why' questions. Children's sites are too numerous to give many recommendations, but as a rule the purely commercial ventures such as barbie.com have limited entertainment value and don't work particularly well, their aim being simply to sell new products. thomasthetankengine.com is an exception – a delight to use, with games and pages to print out and colour and minimal hard sell. bbc.co.uk has pages with games for most of its popular series; disney.co.uk has games and comic-strip stories with music.

However, as you wait for the computer to download and the pieces to click into place, it soon becomes apparent that as yet the web is much less interactive, the gratification it provides much less instant, and its standards of production (including spelling) and content much lower than a book: like a dog walking on its hind legs, the wonder is not how well it does it but that it can do it at all. vw

ADDRESS 39 Whitfield Street, London W1 (020 7681 4200)
OPEN Monday to Friday, 9.00–21.00; Saturday, 10.00–19.00; Sunday, 11.00–19.00
COST £3.00 per half hour
GETTING THERE Goodge Street Underground

Cyberia

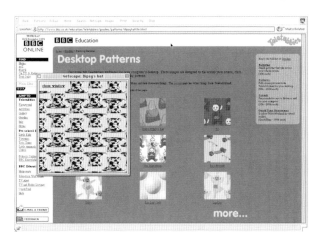

hands-on

London Brass Rubbing Centre

Brass rubbing is the kind of thing that's easy to dismiss as somehow fixed in the late 1960s, stuck in the age of cheese-and-wine parties. But we spent a surprisingly enjoyable hour and a half at the London Brass Rubbing Centre, rubbing a brass of one Sir Thomas Beauchamp, who now has pride of place on my son's bedroom wall. It's good fun for 4s and up provided they have plenty of help from an adult, and the older the child, the more they'll get out of it. You could combine it with a trip to the nearby National Gallery (see page 4.40).

Brasses from British churches commemorate the kings, queens and various aristos of medieval and Tudor times, including plenty of knights in splendid armour. The London Brass Rubbing Centre has copies of many such brasses to choose from, as well as some celtic designs, ranging from small dragons to full-sized figures. Choose the one you like, collect your materials from the cash desk and get rubbing (the Centre is popular with tourists, and can get quite busy). Unless your child is exceptionally neat, it's best to opt for black background paper, since this allows mistakes to be erased. The Crypt Café is right next door.

Anther brass-rubbing venue is All Hallows-by-the-Tower, Byward Street, EC3 (020 7481 2928). JL

ADDRESS The Crypt, St Martin-in-the-Fields Church, Trafalgar Square, London WC2 (020 7930 9306)
OPEN Monday to Saturday, 10.00–18.00; Sunday, 12.00–18.00
COST free admission, but a fee is charged for each rubbing, starting at £2.90 for a small brass, with a reduction of £1 for under-12s
GETTING THERE Charing Cross Underground
BUGGIES yes WHEELCHAIR ACCESS no (steps down to crypt and no lift)

London Recumbents at Dulwich Park

Dulwich Park is a pleasant place for a civilised weekend walk. It has ducks, a boating lake, a café, gardens, a decent playground and some very inquisitive squirrels (and a branch of the ever-reliable PizzaExpress nearby in Dulwich Village). But the best reason to go is London Recumbents and their bikes.

This small, friendly company (you'll find them on the left if you enter the park from College Road) rents out just about every kind of bike you can think of, and some you can't, mostly aimed at families or those with special needs. There are side-by-side trikes, tandems, three-wheelers, hand-cranked tricycles, trailer bikes with carriers for very young children, bikes with baskets for dogs; for the adventurous there are lie-down 'recumbent' bikes, unicycles and even a penny farthing, for which lessons can be booked. Mostly manufactured in Germany or Holland, they are available by the hour or half hour. Children's parties can also be arranged.

We rented a side-by-side tricycle suitable for two very unfit adults (it's called a 'sociable' tandem but, since only one of you can brake and steer, in our case it prompted a bit of back-saddle driving) and a very tough, stable three-wheeler which was ideal for our beginner-cyclist son, giving him a lot of confidence (stabilisers are scorned at London Recumbents). We spent an enjoyable hour trundling around the park's mostly flat paths (you can cycle on most of the main paths though you need to avoid the lake area and the surrounding road on which cars are allowed). London Recumbents also operates from Battersea Park (see page 1.2).JL

ADDRESS Ranger's Yard, Dulwich Park, London SE21 (020 8299 6636)
OPEN usually daily from 9.00 until park closing time (telephone to check)
COST prices start at £3.00 per half hour for a single bike
GETTING THERE West Dulwich rail

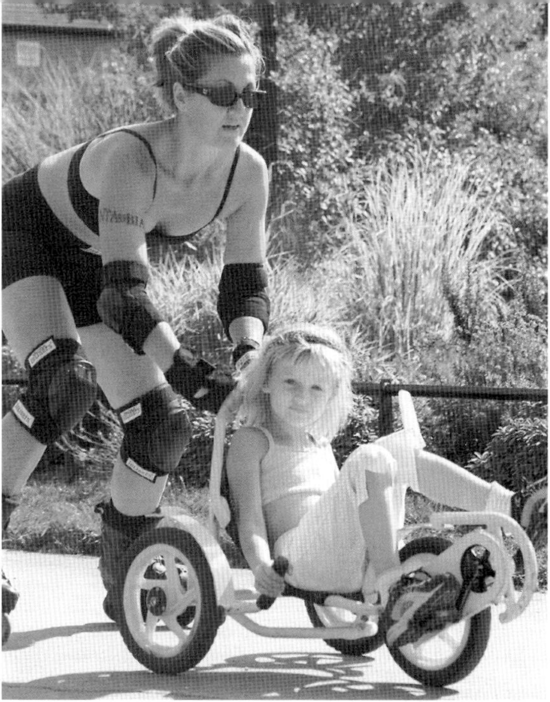

Rucksack Music

Amy Maguire started Rucksack Music, which runs sessions for under-3s and their parents/carers, in 1997, spurred by her disappointment at a badly organised workshop she attended with the children she was minding and dismay at the 'ever-so-British, middle-class accents and high-pitched voices' she found on many commercial tapes. A trained teacher, her aim is to get people into singing with their children again, and she achieves it by making sure parents/carers sing along and enjoy, having as few rules as possible (children are allowed free rein as long as they don't chew the songbooks) and keeping the classes drop-in out of respect for the competing commitments and tight budgets under which many families operate.

Maguire is confident and impressive: she plays piano, guitar and banjo, engages with the children directly, keeps the group moving at a brisk pace, and badgers everyone to sing, play percussion instruments, march, clap and stomp as required (don't go unless you're prepared to be active – this is not a quiet hour of relaxing to soothing music). Longer songs are in the songbooks; otherwise it's 'Wind the Bobbin Up', 'Five Little Speckled Frogs', 'Humpty Dumpty', 'Row, Row the Boat' and the like, ending, of course, with the hokey-cokey. VW

ADDRESS classes every day in various north London venues; telephone 020 8806 9335 or 07957 608151 for details
COST £3.50, concessions £2.50

Toddlers Skating at Alexandra Palace

> You could skate before you could walk, [my mother] would say when I was older. There were white ankle-length boots, at first the smallest the shop at the rink could make ... I think I remember the pushchair, and a snow suit I wore before progressing into a short skating skirt.
> Jenni Diski, *Skating to Antarctica* (Granta Publications, 1977)

I assumed Jenni Diski's claim was poetic licence, especially as my own efforts to be a teenage ice queen had succeeded in little more than attracting local youths keen to have their way with a helpless beginner. But Alexandra Palace ice rink runs two classes for under-5s, with or without an accompanying adult.

We chose the unaccompanied option. And though at first my 4-year-old daughter could barely walk in her ice boots, by the end of the half-hour session she was crossing the rink arms outstretched with only an occasional helping hand and running around to the other side to start again. Children alternately walk across the ice taking small steps, stamping so they get used to the way the blade meets the ground, and slide gripping the teacher's hand. Unlike dance or sports, it's easy to measure personal achievement as you cover more and more ground unaided, and this, combined with the thrill of accomplishing something so patently unnatural and the seedy glamour ice rinks exude, was enough to make it a must-repeat experience. Teacher Michele Langely says she took her own 16-month-old daughter on the ice, though she wouldn't recommend the unqualified to try it with under-2s. Adults who like skating can slip off for a quick turn while their children are being tutored, though you have to be back to meet them after their crossing to take them to the other side to start again. The café in the ice-rink foyer is frankly depressing, but the Alexandra Palace complex offers several other

options, and it's worth planning to spend a bit more time here.

Built in 1873 as the People's Palace, the Ally Pally burned down just 16 days after it was inaugurated, by which time it had already clocked up 124,000 visitors. A new complex opened in 1875 with facilities that included a 12,000-seat Great Hall, a museum, gallery space, banqueting rooms and a theatre. The BBC made the first public television transmission from the eastern part of the building in 1936 and Alexandra Palace was its main transmitting centre until 1956. About half of the palace burned down again in 1980 and has been partially restored.

The complex is depressingly run down or endearingly tatty, depending on your point of view. Certainly the combination of cheap-looking rebuilding and grim fire-scarred areas makes it hard to imagine its former glory, while the mismatch of spaces and activities (the lofty, glass-vaulted ice-rink foyer filled with squat Portakabins) is a good argument against heritage restorations. Facilities include a large playground (no fancy equipment, but plenty of seating and space to run around), a large boating lake with a small café, large deer and donkey enclosures and a very large park (80 hectares). There's more than enough space here for children to run around in safety; we based ourselves on the slope behind the rose garden, which leads to a pretty wooded area that's well worth exploring.

The Phoenix pub offers a bar menu from burgers to humus as well as a children's menu and restaurant-standard meals (swordfish and salsa, for instance) at reasonable prices. There's copious seating outdoors, next to the terrace from which you get a fantastic view of the clustered roofs of Muswell Hill and Archway with a backdrop that includes the Post Office Tower, St Paul's, Canary Wharf and the Millennium Dome (there are telescopes for the dedicated), or you can sit in the kitsch Palm Court, where giant trees tower over sphinxes, obelisk lamp-posts, pyramid foun-

Toddlers Skating at Alexandra Palace

tains and Sega gamestations. The Popcorn in the Park café in the Grove occupies a wonderfully funky desert-island-style hut with tacked-on verandas and doors in the shape of stencilled trees. It serves homemade vegan food and Italian ice cream – 'no cards, no cappuccino, no cheques, no candy, no crisps, no junk' – with menus from as far afield as Trinidad, Thailand and Tanzania (the alliteration's catching) on different days. It's run on a voluntary basis for Mencap and is the kind of place I'd like to support, but we found the strictures about filling in your own order card, not complaining if you have to wait and not asking for any variations on the set menu off-putting, and in any case, they don't accept £20 notes, which was all I had. The Islands, beyond the café, is a similarly funky playhut and outdoor area open from 13.00 to 16.00 for under-5s and their carers. Among the many special events the Alexandra Palace hosts is an annual children's funfair beside the ice rink, open daily from 12.00 to 19.00 in the summer holidays. And if you want to hone your child's skating skills between weekday lessons you'll also be able to try out Kiddies Kingdom, a collection of inflatables in the ice-rink foyer from 11.00 to 16.30, weekends and school holidays. VW

ADDRESS Alexandra Palace, Alexandra Palace Way, London N22 (020 8365 2121)
OPEN Tuesdays in termtime, 12.30 (accompanied); 16.00 (unaccompanied)
COST £2.50 (including skate hire and entrance to the public session for adult and child in accompanied class)
GETTING THERE Wood Green Underground, then bus W3, Alexandra Palace rail from Moorgate (weekdays only) or King's Cross; free car park outside ice-rink entrance

Waterfront Leisure Centre

As leisure pools go, Wild 'n Wet at the Waterfront has it all: a scary, pitch-dark 65-metre-long anaconda slide that snakes outside the building, a five-lane slide, a Jacuzzi, a wave machine, a mushroom-shaped spray you can dive underneath, a waterfall and the next-door Rascals Adventure Centre, a tame version of Bramley's Big Adventure (see page 7.6). The L-shaped pool has a shallow area you swim into under a wooden bridge and there's a separate pool for under-8s with games around the sides. It looks good – a bright, lofty space with jungle pictures, fake rocks and greenery, a bamboo hut, a jeep, and crocodiles and turtles lurking in the water – but you're not allowed to climb on the poolside turtle or the hippo fountain in the under-8s pool and the hut is not for play but contains machinery.

Like many leisure centres, the Waterfront operates a bookable crèche and offers lessons including baby swimming, which is good for giving you confidence in handling something so slippery-when-wet. The upstairs café scores highly, and there's pleasure to be had from watching the river flow by outside and the loading of the Woolwich Ferry – a free car and pedestrian service (every 10 minutes between 6.00 and 20.00 Monday to Saturday and 11.30 and 19.30 on Sundays) and unexpected urban delight, with views of the Thames Barrier – which connects with the North Woolwich Old Station Museum (see page 3.22). VW

ADDRESS High Street, Woolwich, London SE18 (020 8317 5000)
OPEN Wild 'n Wet: termtime 15.00–20.00; weekends and holidays 10.00–13.00 and 14.00–20.00; Rascals: Monday to Friday, 9.30–18.00; weekends 9.30–14.00
COST Wild 'n Wet: adults £2.95, children £2.10 (offpeak); adults £3.80, children £2.80 (peak); Rascals: £3.10 (additional children £1.10)
GETTING THERE Woolwich Dockyard rail; car park

Yogabugs

Fenella Lindsell had the idea of Yogabugs after observing the pleasure and relief from anxiety her stepson derived from joining in with yoga practice with her and her partner. In 1996 she co-founded the Art of Health, which also runs classes in baby massage (see page 7.4) and music for under-3s alongside adult yoga (mothers can bring pre-crawling babies to some sessions), Ta'i Chi and a range of complementary treatments and therapies.

At the class I observed, a group of boisterous boys aged between 5 and 7 followed with rapt attention teacher Vicky Mitchell's inventive stories about bumpy camel rides, encounters with cobras and a mountain where greedy people go gold-digging – each designed to incorporate several yoga positions. At the end, as they lay in the 'corpse' position and were told to imagine themselves on a warm beach breathing in time to the waves, my very relaxed daughter nearly fell asleep.

Different yoga positions are beneficial for medical conditions from asthma to constipation, and it is agreed that regular sessions help hyperactivity and poor sleep patterns, but the real point of Yogabugs is to provide an enjoyable, non-competitive physical activity that will help children from 3 to 8 to delight in their own flexibility and become aware of their bodies' potential.

Adults can enjoy pre-booked half-hour sessions of aromatherapy, head-and-shoulder massage or reflexology while classes are on. VW

ADDRESS The Art of Health, 280 Balham High Road, London SW17 (020 8682 1800)
OPEN Wednesday, 16.15–1700; Sunday, 11.00–11.45
COST £3.50
GETTING THERE Tooting Bec Underground; free parking in side streets

watching

Arsenal Ladies

If you're put off by the expense and near-unobtainability of Premier League tickets, the fact that the players earn more per match than your annual salary and male football supporters' reputation for drunken violence, try Arsenal Ladies. The crowd for the home match against Ilkeston Town LFC numbered about 60 – a far cry from the 90,000 who cheered the USA's women's team to its 1999 World Cup victory – but half of those were children: 2–5s who amused themselves by climbing the steps and playing with the seats in the safe, enclosed terrace; a group of 6- to 8-year-olds, boys and girls, who ran up and down alongside the pitch and enthusiastically compared signed programmes; and teenage girls who watched with rapt attention. Half-time refreshments included chips, veggie burgers and hot dogs as well as Bovril.

Play was slow but committed, and despite the frequent shouts of 'Man-on, Clare!', the game was all Arsenal's. Like the men's team, Arsenal Ladies has a big effective centre-half in Carol Harwood and two fast over-lapping wing-backs in Clare Wheatley and Kirsty Pealling, who gave a particularly fine performance but was booked near the end for 'reacting in an aggressive manner to the opposition'. They also have a muscular centre-forward in England international Marianne Spacey. The team was formed in 1987 and has won four WFA Cups and been National Premier League champions three times. Word on the terraces was that this wasn't a very good game, but at 6-0, it's the result that counts. VW

ADDRESS Borehamwood FC, Broughinge Road, Borehamwood
TIME Sundays, 14.00 (telephone 020 7704 4147 for fixture list)
COST £2; children free
GETTING THERE A1 to Borehamwood; turn right at the first major roundabout on to Brook Road; Broughinge Road is the first right

BFI London Imax

The British Film Institute's shiny new Imax cinema, which opened in 1999 in what was once Waterloo's cardboard city, boasts the largest screen in the country and promises 'mind-trip' 2-D and 3-D cinema.

The building is a towering glass-covered cylinder, seven storeys tall. Unfortunately, big doesn't always mean exciting, and some of the few films made for this technology err on the side of worthy. Our first visit was to see a 2-D film about space exploration which was flat in every sense of the word. A 3-D film about sea creatures was much more fun. Equipped with special specs (available in children's sizes) we were immersed in an undersea world, with sharks, octopuses, sea lions and jellyfish seeming to swim out of the screen towards us. Even better was the cartoon trailer which demonstrated the potential this technology has for animation.

Choose your film carefully and the Imax can be edge-of-your-seat fun. Children need to be at least 4 to enjoy it, and those prone to travel sickness should be wary of any especially vivid action shots which can cause a slight sense of nausea.

You can also see 3-D films at the Pepsi Imax Cinema in the Trocadero, Piccadilly (020 7494 4153); the screen there is smaller and the 3-D glasses less comfortable, but it's an enjoyable experience nevertheless. JL

ADDRESS 1 Charlie Chaplin Walk, South Bank, London SE1
020 7902 1234
COST prices vary according to film; under-5s free, family ticket available
GETTING THERE Waterloo rail or Underground
BUGGIES can be left in foyer
WHEELCHAIR ACCESS yes; also audio descriptions for blind and partially sighted, induction loop for hard of hearing

Cats

A less likely starting point for a hit musical than the poetry of T S Eliot – symbol of highbrow intellectualism, and dead to boot – is hard to imagine. But *Cats* is now in its twentieth year, has been staged in 122 productions worldwide and has grossed £1.3 billion. Andrew Lloyd Webber, who had to remortgage his house to raise the last £50,000 of the £0.5 million start-up costs, must be laughing all the way to the bank.

Eliot's poems – published in October 1939 as *Old Possum's Book of Practical Cats* – are essentially a collection of character studies which the musical strings together by means of a very un-Eliot-like skeleton plot in which the Jellicle tribe is gathered to choose which of its members will journey to the Heavyside Layer in the sky to be reborn into a new life. The music is pleasantly varied, the dancing sharp and powerful and the lyrics obviously cogent – apart from the execrable hit 'Memory', cobbled together by Trevor Nunn (who should know better) from fragments of other Eliot poems. So is there any point in worrying about the messages the 700 or so children who see *Cats* on a matinee day are receiving?

Probably not, but I do. First, Eliot's poems are casually racist, with references to 'chinks' that could have been designed to offend the tourists who pack the theatre – surely the irreverence to the spirit of the poems could have extended occasionally to the letter? Second, the material is thoroughly sexist: the tribe's leader Old Deuteronomy is revered and respected, his age conferring status and wisdom, whereas his contemporary Grizabella, a female who left the tribe for adventures in the outside world, is got up like a faded Hollywood starlet whom age has made ridiculous. And the Jellicles are a malicious, blinkered and bigoted lot, rejecting Grizabella because she chose to explore her options (though it is she in the end who is chosen by Old Deuteronomy to ascend and be reborn in cat heaven – punishment or prize?).

Cats

Nevertheless, my daughter sat on the edge of her seat throughout, and though some of Eliot's 1930s stereotypes (the portly, spat-sporting man-about-town Bustopher Jones or the aged actor Gus) surely mean little to today's youngsters, others translate well, in particular rude-boy Rum Tum Tugger who struts his stuff convincingly, the mischievous duo Mungojerrie and Rumpleteazer and the athletic conjuror Mr Mistofelees. And the staging is full of excitement, the cats emerging through tunnels by the front row and engaging physically with the audience, not to mention the moment the lights go out …

We also took the backstage tour, which allowed us to squeeze into the prompt box, crawl through the cats' tunnels, take to the stage and stand below it where the crew manipulate the scenery, opening and shutting the 3-ton car boot and shooting actor Steven Wayne, ironically the only surviving member of the original cast, out through a trapdoor which he opens with the force of his head at 5 kph (he wears a crash helmet under his wig). These cats don't have nine lives, and mistimings could be fatal.

The theatre also runs a Kids Club for over-5s on the first Saturday in the month from September to Christmas that includes drama and make-up workshops. Education officer John Scarborough is very approachable, and his team go out of their way to respond to individual fans' dreams. vw

ADDRESS New London Theatre, Drury Lane, London wc2
(020 7405 0072; tours 020 7400 5005)
OPEN evening performances 19.45; Tuesday and Saturday matinee 15.00
COST performances: £10.50–£35; tours: adults £3.50, children £2.50
GETTING THERE Covent Garden, Holborn Underground
BUGGIES not recommended on tours
WHEELCHAIR ACCESS by arrangement

Cinema Clubs

Who said the Saturday morning picture show was dead? Young cinephiles are increasingly well catered for in London, with a growing number of cinema clubs for children and families. These clubs show films – from the latest Disney blockbusters to old favourites such as Thunderbirds, Wombles and Muppets, or sci-fi classics – suitable for a range of age groups. Most offer something more too – themed activities before the film, question-and-answer sessions afterwards, competitions, prizes, newsletters, badges, ticket perks and so on (and newspapers and coffee for accompanying adults if you're really lucky). Quite a few also give members the opportunity to visit the projection room and start the film if it's their birthday. Membership and ticket prices are usually very reasonable, and day membership is generally available. Most clubs have similar rules, governed by law: adults are not allowed unless accompanying a child; children aged 5 or over can be left to watch the film alone, though carers must be around to collect them afterwards; children under 7 won't be admitted to a PG-certificate film unless accompanied by an adult.

Here we list film clubs and cinemas regularly showing family films:

THE BARBICAN: CHILDREN'S CINEMA CLUB
London EC2 (box office 020 7638 8891)
Set up a decade ago, the Barbican Children's Cinema Club (originally called the Splodge Club) can lay claim to being the first of these clubs. For 5- to 11-year-olds, it shows a children's or family-friendly film on Saturdays at 11.00. Once a month there are 'Saturday Special' activities in the pit foyer – a demonstration of Thai dancing to coincide with a showing of *The King and I*, for example, or a Mad Hatter's Tea Party for *Alice in Wonderland*. As well as the typical blockbusters, the club also makes a point of showing children's classic and foreign films, sometimes

with a translator. At the time of writing, there were plans to bring along film critics to talk to the children, and to introduce a movie-making trolley to provide activities along the lines of the art carts found in many galleries.

Tickets £2.50 (adults £3.00), annual membership £4, day membership 50p. Members receive a card and badge, and can bring up to three paying guests.

CLAPHAM PICTURE HOUSE: KIDS CLUB
Venn Street, London SW4 (020 7498 2242)
One of the jolliest film clubs we've come across. Children can be found in the bar on Saturday mornings, splashing paint around or making masks, rockets and so on for half an hour before the movie begins. Questions and answers, competitions – and prizes – follow the film. For parents, there's a row of good cafés opposite the cinema.

Begins every Saturday at 11.15 (film at 11.45). Tickets £2.00, annual membership £3.00. Day membership available.

NATIONAL FILM THEATRE: JUNIOR NFT
South Bank, London SE1 (020 7928 3232)
Not exactly a club, but every month there is a themed season of children's films shown on Saturdays and Sundays – for example a 'Puffin on Screen' season during which films based on books published by Puffin are screened. (For the over-7s, there are also half-term activities and workshops to tie in with movie themes.)

Tickets usually £2, (adults £6.20) with reductions for British Film Institute members. Membership not essential.

Cinema Clubs

PHOENIX CINEMA: THE PHOENIX FREDDIES
52 High Road, London N2 (020 8444 6789)
Film-based activities for 6- to 12-year-olds – drawing storyboards or exploring the cinema, for example – begin every Saturday at 11.00, with the film starting at noon. An interesting selection of films and themes – such as, *It Came From Outer Space* during sci-fi month. Members receive a membership card, badge and 'The Fred File'. Tickets are £1.50 for activity session and film for members (£3 for non-members), adults pay £1.50 for film. Annual membership £15 (£9 for siblings). (It is possible to hold children's parties here – with film screening.)

RIO CINEMA: SATURDAY MORNING PICTURE CLUB
107 Kingsland High Street, London E8 (020 7241 9410)
Every Saturday. Doors open at 10.30 and the film begins at 11.00. Tickets are £2.00 for children, £3.00 for accompanying adults. Membership free. The films shown are mostly a mix of U or PG recent releases. At the time of writing there were also half-term matinees and 'Playcentre' matinees on Tuesdays.

RITZY CINEMA: FILMS FOR KIDS
Coldharbour Lane, London SW2 (020 7737 2121)
Shows a children's film – of the *Babe, Prince of Egypt* variety – every Saturday at 10.30. Accompanying adults are provided with free coffee in the Ritzy café. Tickets £1 for children, £2 for adults.

STRATFORD PICTURE HOUSE: KIDS CLUB
Gerry Raffles Square, Salway Road, London E15 (020 8555 3366; programme information 020 8855 3311)

Cinema Clubs

Every Saturday morning. Doors open at 10.30 for activities – colouring-in, mask-making, potato prints, etc – with the film following at 11.00. Most of the films are for the younger audience, though you'll also get the occasional Batman or Star Trek movie. Special events are held at Christmas and on the cinema's birthday in August. Tickets £2.00 members (£2.50 non-members). Annual membership £5 (day membership 50p).

TRICYCLE CINEMA
269 Kilburn High Road, London NW6 (box office 020 7328 1000; film information 020 7328 1900)
Shows 'family films' every Saturday at 13.00. Children under 7 must be accompanied by a paying adult. Tickets £3 for children, £4 adults.

The James Baldwin studio can be hired for children's parties when booked in conjunction with a Saturday film show.

VIRGIN HAMMERSMITH: KIDS CLUB
207 King Street, London W6 (box office 020 8748 2388 for programme information; 020 8970 6026 for advance booking)
Every Saturday from 10.00 to 12.00. Children's and adults' tickets £2.00 (including 'brat snack'). Mostly U- or PG-certificate films ranging from Wind in the Willows to Men in Black.
JL

Half Moon Young People's Theatre

The Half Moon puts as much effort into encouraging children's participation outside the auditorium as within. The theatre develops programmes with local schools, runs six different weekly workshops for 8- to 25-year-olds – for a fee of £1 – that focus on technical, creative and performance skills, and takes on 17 trainee technicians and workshop leaders each year.

Saturdays are largely devoted to 3- to 8-year-olds, when the theatre runs workshops linked where possible to performances, many of which reflect its remit to 'celebrate the cultural diversity of London'. The aim here, according to artistic director Chris Elwell, is to 'get them hooked young', in the hope they'll follow through into the older children's schemes. Appropriately, we attended 'Meeting Mermaids', in which tutor Danni Walsh, assisted by YPT trainee Amma Nkrumah and ten children, helped Mirabelle the mermaid to find her lost treasure, followed by a performance of *The Mermaid's Tale*. The workshop was imaginative and thoroughly appreciated, and both Danni and Amma chatted to parents and children in the break before the performance (bring sandwiches – the only refreshments on site are two vending machines with sweets, crisps and drinks).

Other dedicated children's theatres include the Polka (240 The Broadway, London SW19, 020 8543 4888) which has two performance spaces, one specialising in under-6s, and the Unicorn Theatre at the Pleasance (Carpenter's Mews, North Road, London N7, 020 7607 1800). VW

ADDRESS 43 White Horse Road, London E1 (020 7265 9994)
OPEN Saturday workshops 12.30; performances 14.00
COST workshops: £2.50; performances: £4, concessions £3
GETTING THERE Limehouse DLR

Puppet Theatre Barge

The Puppet Theatre Barge has been cruising the canals and the Thames between Little Venice and Abingdon since 1981. The company produces one new show a year (for adults or children) using marrionettes, shadow puppets and rod puppets accompanied by a recorded soundtrack.

'Children don't attend on their own, so our aim is to entertain adults too,' says co-founder Juliet Rogers, who adapts most of the plays. She uses an eclectic mix of source material – whether fairy tales such as *The Three Little Pigs* or *Captain Grimey*, which she worked up into a half-hour performance from a couple of unattributed paragraphs found in an anthology, or a shadowplay she developed from a story she made up for her grandchildren. Unlike many puppet productions at the Little Angel Theatre (14 Dagmar Passage, London N1), children aren't talked down to here: tales have a distinct political spin (*Captain Grimey* deals adeptly with pollution and attitudes to physical difference), and the astute characterisation is helped along by original songs and realistic dialogue voiced by professional actors. And there's no reluctance to give hand-me-down stories a full makeover if that's what Rogers thinks her audience would prefer, as with the three little pigs, all of whom save their bacon.

Painted red and yellow and festooned with bunting, the barge offers the added delight of watching ducks and boats float by through the low-level portholes. The company also puts on evening performances for adults – following *Macbeth*, how about a puppet *L'Atalante*? vw

ADDRESS November to June: Blomfield Road, Little Venice, London W9 (020 7249 6876/0836 202 745)
COST adults £6, children and concessions £5.50
GETTING THERE Warwick Avenue Underground
WHEELCHAIR ACCESS by arrangement

Zippos Circus

Two hundred years ago, in the centre of London, Major Phillip Astley rode a horse around a ring and the circus was born. Zippos, which has been touring some 35 London venues since 1987, is very much a traditional affair, its unlikely alliance with the National Childbirth Trust and assurances of animal-friendly practices notwithstanding. The atmosphere is exciting from the moment you enter the big top – just smell the sawdust – and though the disco lights and plush red curtains seem old-fashioned and tacky, that's the point. This is not the Billy Smart's spectacular you might remember from childhood television; the big top is actually quite small, and you're close to the action in a crowd with the same sense of anticipation and involvement as at a football match.

The show changes each year, as Martin 'Zippo' Burton scours the world for new acts, though there are some core performers including clowns Rusty, Tweedy and PORG Little Nick. The whole is presided over by Alexis – white-faced, in a series of ever more elaborate costumes the late Liberace would have killed for – and the spirit is akin to pantomime with slapstick, cross-dressing, camp and audience participation. Some of the acts make you wonder how anyone ever thought of doing something so absurd. Yet at its best it's breathtaking: Beautiful Amanda suspended by one leg from a swathe of white cloth, circling the ring faster and faster; Saina, pushing the trapeze ever higher; the death-defying dancing on the high wire. Unlike dancers, the corps de ballet at least are neither particularly graceful nor uniform – you get the impression you too could run away and find a place here. vw

TIMES AND VENUES call 07050 121416 for details
WEBSITE www.zipposcircus.co.uk
COST adults £12/£8.50/£5.50, children over 2 £10/£6.50/£3.50

eating

Bank Restaurant and Bar

Bank is that rare treat: a proper, civilised restaurant which – at least during weekend brunch – makes children welcome.

The Julyan Wickham-designed interior is a cool, elegant and very grown-up mix of mirrors, murals and planes of colour. Staff, immaculate in black, are endlessly patient – in our case in the face of some pretty trying behaviour from a terrible twosome of almost-4-year-olds.

The food, like everything else, is classy. Arriving a bit late for the eggs Benedict/full English breakfast-type brunch (which is the best time to come with kids), we indulged in a three-course lunch, between us trying out the Caesar salad, paprika-encrusted red snapper, fishcake, fennel and herb risotto, fresh fruit salad, various ice creams and tiramisu. The children chose tagliatelle and some very superior fish and chips from the children's menu (other options were chipolatas, barbecued chicken or beef burger, with chips or mash).

We had collected colouring books, building bricks and so on at reception, though the combination of crayons, white linen tablecloths and immaculately painted walls made for some indigestible moments. In any event, the crayons and colouring books proved less interesting than the automatic taps in the toilets, which for some reason were judged to be hugely entertaining, demanding several visits to the loo.

There are excellent baby-changing facilities and disabled toilets. Highchairs are available. We spent on average £35 per adult (including coffee, service and wine) and £9 per child. Not cheap, but a real treat. JL

ADDRESS 1 Kingsway, Aldwych, London WC2 (020 7234 3344)
OPEN family-friendly brunch Saturday and Sunday, 11.30–15.30
GETTING THERE Covent Garden Underground

The Rainforest Cafe

Predictably, you enter and exit the Rainforest Cafe through the shop. But at least you'll know by your reaction to the talking tree giving facts about the world's rainforests whether or not to proceed with the experience. If yes, then it's downstairs to a series of cavernous rooms hung with plastic greenery. At sporadic intervals life-size gorillas beat their chests, giant butterflies flap their wings, and – despite the organisation's claim to 'educate' – a treetop leopard miles from home growls and waves its tail. The calypso soundtrack is punctuated by claps of thunder, bird and animal cries and the roar of the waterfall. We loved it.

Staff are more than helpful, supplying highchairs and responding to our request to be moved nearer to the aquarium (the fish, at least, are real) with a genuine 'whatever's best for you'. You can't eat cheaply here – main courses are £10.95–£14.95, sandwiches £6.75–£8.95 and the Rainforest Rascals menu £7.95 for a main course and dessert, while an apple juice will set you back £2.55 – but portions are substantial. The cappuccino is insufferably bland, but everything else went down well.

The company raises funding through customer donations for organisations working for rainforest conservation. Was it that no mention was made of donating a share of the profits, the processed nature of the food, or just that I felt sorry for the three parrots whose existence is divided between the shop and a specially created indoor habitat that made me feel its commitment is little more than a convenient gimmick? VW

ADDRESS 20 Shaftesbury Avenue, London W1 (020 7434 3111)
OPEN Monday to Thursday, 12.00–22.30; Friday, 12.00–23.30; Saturday, 11.30–24.00; Sunday, 11.30–22.30. Booking recommended
GETTING THERE Piccadilly Circus Underground
WHEELCHAIR ACCESS by arrangement

Smollensky's on the Strand

At Smollensky's you can get a very decent steak sandwich, pasta dish, Caesar salad or such like, while most children will be happy with pizza, fish fingers, chicken nuggets, spaghetti or burgers, fruit 'koktails' (we particularly like the 'Spiderman' one) and chips, chips, chips.

But of course the appeal of Smollensky's isn't really the food. On Saturday and Sunday lunchtimes (and some bank holidays), this relaxingly lit American bar/restaurant, tucked rather unpromisingly down a flight of steps off the busy Strand, pulls out all the stops to keep the kids – and therefore their parents/carers – happy. There are Nintendo games to plug into and TV screens showing cartoons, while near the bar are Tiny Tikes trucks, cars and planes for smaller children to play on (though they must be supervised here, as elsewhere in the restaurant).

It's a good idea to arrive around 12.30–13.00 because the entertainments – including typically a clown or a magician who will do tricks at your table, face painting (£2.50 extra), a free raffle and perhaps a puppet show – are usually laid on from then until 15.00. Highchairs are available, as are balloons and sparklers.

As you'd expect, the atmosphere is relaxed, there are no disapproving diners at the next table, and there always seems to be at least one child behaving worse than your own. Meals cost £20–£25 per adult for three courses without wine, and £8.50 per child. Booking not always necessary but advisable. JL

ADDRESS 105 The Strand, London WC2 (020 7497 2101)
OPEN children's lunch Saturday and Sunday, 12.00–15.00
GETTING THERE Charing Cross Underground
BUGGIES can be left at reception (steps down to the restaurant)

eating

Tiger Lil's

Tiger Lil's introduces the 1990s holy grail of interactivity to the restaurant. No longer a passive consumer content to choose from a pre-set menu, here you select your ingredients, design your dishes and supervise their cooking.

About 30 different items or combinations of various degrees of exoticism – celery and radish, red chard and sugar-snap peas, black-eyed beans, cloud-ear fungus, beansprouts and corn, tofu, fried bean curd, mussels and squid, wind-dried sausage, beef, chicken and pork – are arranged on a counter with the ones that require the most cooking at the end. You pile up what you want and take it to one of the wokpeople, who tosses it around with the sauce (oyster, teriyaki, satay, etc) and garnishes your order. Repeat the process until you can eat no more. The pyrotechnics, as flames shoot up from the woks sometimes to ceiling height, are dramatic – dress lightly as the place heats up very quickly.

The atmosphere is informal, the decor unpretentious, and the many children obviously loved it. My advice is to limit the ingredients and go for smaller helpings (even when busy the queues are never more than a few minutes). Rice is brought to your table; there is a limited selection of beer and wine at reasonable prices; highchairs on request. VW

ADDRESS 16a Clapham Common Southside, London SW4 (020 7720 5433)/500 Kings Road, London SW10 (020 7376 5003)/270 Upper Street, London N1 (020 7226 1118)
OPEN Monday to Friday, 12.00–15.00 and 18.00–23.30; Saturday, 12.00–24.00; Sunday, 12.00–23.00. Booking advisable
COST £11 not including drinks; £5.50 for under-10s
GETTING THERE Clapham South/Fulham Broadway/Highbury & Islington Underground

Yo! Sushi

The sushi conveyor belt – a concept devised in Japan in the 1960s – is the hallmark of the Yo! Sushi chain. It's also a constant source of inter-active entertainment for children – this is self-service with a difference – and a welcome change from the all-too-usual pizzas and burgers.

The food – maki rolls, salmon nigiri, sashimi, sushi and so on – trundles around a central preparation area. Sitting at the counter on bar stools or at tables, you simply pick out the dishes you want as they parade by. Press a tap at the counter for refills of water, or grab a can or bottle from the robot drinks trolley – a source of great fascination for my son – as it pooters about the place.

Plates are colour-coded for price (£1.50–£3.50 each): at the end of your meal your waiter tots up the stacked empties to calculate the bill. It's possible to eat quite reasonably – lunch for four for around £40, say – but beware: it's all such fun that it's also possible to get carried away and notch up a far bigger bill than you expected. We originally visited on the recommendation of our friend Max, a 7-year-old sushi fan, who has been known to eat his way through £30.

For picky young eaters, there are some easy-going children's specials. Look out for the Yo! You Kids plates with dishes such as prawn cocktail, mini tuna or salmon nigiri, cheese and pickle rolls, rice balls and chicken teriyaki. Also popular with children are the fruit options – kiwi, banana, melon – and the sweet pancakes. Clearly Yo! Sushi is keen to get them young – its merchandising includes a Yo! Sushi yo-yo and Yo! babygro.

We ate at the Poland Street branch (don't be put off by all those Soho media types), but there are other Yo! Sushis at Harvey Nichols in Knightsbridge (020 7235 5000), Selfridges Food Hall in Oxford Street (020 7318 3895), in the central arena of the Millennium Dome, and at the O2 Centre (255 Finchley Road, London NW3, 020 7431 4499).

Yo! Sushi

The O2 Centre is itself a fun place to visit: above the ground-floor Sainsbury's are two tiers of shops (including a branch of Books etc) and restaurants surrounding aquaria housing exotic fish, a central mountain of fake stone, a waterfall and a bubble lift. In addition to Yo! Sushi there are branches of Ed's Easy Diner, which provides entertainment in the form of activity sheets and table juke-boxes, Babe Ruth's, where you can watch live sport or take five-minute turns in the ball room, and Capital Radio Café, where the DJ runs competitions throughout the day. The centre also houses the London International Gallery of Children's Art (Tuesday to Thursday, 16.00–18.00; Saturday and Sunday, 12.00–18.00) and runs a crèche at weekends, 10.00–17.00 (£1.75 per half hour for a maximum of two hours). JL

ADDRESS 52 Poland Street, London W1 (020 7287 0443)
OPEN daily, 12.00–24.00
GETTING THERE Piccadilly Circus Underground

shopping

Bookshops

London's bookshops underwent something of a revolution in the 1990s – so much so that we now take for granted the comfy-sofa, cappuccino-bar atmosphere in which our children can sprawl on the carpet and thumb through/read/chew the books without getting dirty looks from the sales staff. Central London's two biggest bookshops – Borders in Oxford Street and Waterstone's in Piccadilly – both offer an extensive, excellent range of children's books in laidback and welcoming surroundings.

First **Waterstone's** (203–206 Piccadilly, London W1), Europe's largest bookshop and London's swishest, which opened in the famous old Simpsons store in 1999. Its children's department on the second floor is bright and inviting, featuring a touch-screen computer, a box of dressing-up clothes for the kids, and sofas for exhausted parents. Books are easy to access: reference books, for example, are divided not only by age group but also by categories such as 'Egyptians', 'Space', 'Beasts'; bestsellers and new books are well displayed; and suggestions for future reading – 'If you like Harry Potter, try these' – are made. Children will like the fishtank in the adjoining juice bar. There are toilets and a parent-and-baby room. The lifts are so slow you're better off with the stairs. Weekend events – book readings or meet-the-Lego-expert sessions, for instance – are often held, so telephone for details. Waterstone's Piccadilly is open Monday to Saturday, 8.30–23.00; Sunday, 12.00–18.00.

At **Borders** (203 Oxford Street, London W1), meanwhile, you'll find everything from toddlers' board books to fiction for young adults, plus a comprehensive 'family issues' section – death, divorce, gay dads, dog heaven, you name it – and videos and story tapes. Carpeted sit-on steps, tables and chairs encourage browsing. Alongside is a café which, though its coffee is distinctly so-so, allows you to sit and watch Oxford Street bustle by outside. Borders stages children's events – a Mog tea party or

Dr Xargle storytime session, for instance – usually on Sunday afternoons or during school holidays (telephone for details or pick up an events leaflet at the store). The children's department is on the second floor (where there are also toilets and baby-changing facilities). Open Monday to Saturday, 8.00–23.00; Sunday, 12.00–18.00. There is another branch of Borders at 120 Charing Cross Road, WC2, though the children's department here is less impressive.

Not to be overshadowed by the Borders-style giants, London also has a number of small (sometimes very small) but excellent specialist children's bookshops. A prime example is **The Lion and the Unicorn** (19 King Street, Richmond) which is so tiny and busy it turns bookbuying into a contact sport. It's been going for more than two decades and it's packed with an excellent selection of children's books for 0 to teens. Behind the counter are posters and signed photographs of authors who have visited the shop for readings and signings over the years: Johnny Morris, Roald Dahl, Mike Rosen, Terry Jones, Shirley Hughes, Lynne Reid Banks, Helen Cooper ... Staff are helpful and knowledgeable. When I asked for a book to introduce a young child to the idea of a new baby, I was instantly presented with six options; the assistant, who clearly kept an in-depth filing system in her head, knew exactly where each one was on the shelves. As I queued to pay for my books (rather more of them than I had intended), two buggy-pushing mothers were chatting in front of me. 'I love this shop,' said one of them. 'So do I,' replied her friend, 'I spend a fortune here.' Open Monday to Friday, 9.30–17.30; Saturday, 9.30–18.00 (closed on Sunday except in the run-up to Christmas).

Endearingly small and slightly untidy, the Tardis-like **Books for Children** (97 Wandsworth Bridge Road, London SW6) was established in 1989 by Diana Wolfe Murray, a grandmother of six who clearly knows

what children like. Her extensive stock, which is packed into two floors, ranges from picture books for the very young to novels for teen readers, plus a good choice of audio books. It's a well-chosen combination of old favourites and new writing. Despite the shop's small size, somehow there's room for a few toys and children's chairs. The policy is to let children wander around and pick up books – 'We want them to enjoy the books.' Staff are interested, enthusiastic and helpful, and aim to read all the books themselves. They will order books that aren't in stock – and books for adults too. Open Monday, 10.00–18.00; Tuesday to Friday, 9.30–18.00; Saturday, 9.30–17.30.

Bigger, bustling and just as friendly, **The Children's Book Centre** (237 Kensington High Street, London W8) has more than 20,000 titles in stock for children from 0 to 13. The range – fiction and non-fiction – is impressive. Reference books for parents and children cover every issue from pregnancy to racism, bereavement and visiting the dentist; the religious section featured books on Islam, Sikhism, Hinduism and Judaism among others and there's an excellently comprehensive selection of material about the human body. The endorsements lining the walls – from authors such as Colin McNaughton, Susanna Gretz and Shirley Hughes (as well as one from John Major) – seem well deserved. The shop also stocks toys (see page 10.22). Open Monday to Wednesday, Friday, Saturday, 9.30–18.30; Thursday 9.30–19.00; Sunday, 12.00–18.00. JL/VW

Covent Garden

Covent Garden is packed with entertainment in addition to its museums (see pages 3.12, 4.14 and 4.66) – James Street usually has living-statue mime artists and musicians, The Market musicians and street theatre, and even the workaday dry cleaners/shoe-repair shop on the corner of High Holborn and Shaftesbury Avenue boasts a cobbler automaton. The largely car-free streets, plentiful places to eat, market and shops to cater for all budgets make this a pleasant day out.

Our favourite specialist shop among many, Oriental stockists **Neal Street East** (5 Neal Street) is an Aladdin's cave of cheap treasures. The ground-floor bookshop has a small children's section that stocks fact, fiction and fairy tales from Asia and Africa, but the highlight is the basement Bazaar, crammed with basket after basket of inexpensive toys. Among the articulated snakes, clockwork mice, fairy wands, fans, kaleidoscopes, key rings, magic slates, musical instruments, rubber frogs and walking dogs are more unusual items such as Japanese water flowers and magic tricks. There are more than 100 toys at under £1.50 and dozens for much less.

Other specialist Covent Garden shops include the **Kite Store** (48 Neal Street), which has single-line kites for over-2s from £7.75 and steerable two-line kites for over-5s from £9.95. Advice is free and forthcoming and the shop also stocks books, magazines and yo-yos. **The London Dolls House Co** (29 The Market) is more like a museum than a shop: it does have paper kits for around £20 and Le Toy Van furniture for around £15 per room, but the average house price is nearer £500, with the Art Deco Ocean Liner House retailing at a cool £2450 and a miniature Rietveld Red/Blue chair at £255. **Benjamin Pollock's Toy Shop** (44 The Market) specialises in puppets, hand-made toys, model theatres and paper-doll books (look out for Pope John Paul II). **Eric Snook** (32 The Market) has

a good range of wooden, soft and kinetic toys from dancing flowers to battery-operated spiders, plus London souvenirs. **Peter Rabbit & Friends** (42 The Market) stocks every imaginable object in Peter Rabbit, Winnie the Pooh, Paddington or Wallace and Gromit form (check out the Wallace and Gromit air freshener). **The Tintin Shop** (34 Floral Street) has clothes, books, tapes, jigsaws and collectibles. And there are also branches of Hamley's and The Disney Store (see page 10.24).

The **Dorling Kindersley Bookshop** (10–13 King Street) unfortunately fails to reflect the child-friendly nature of this publisher's products, though its range of information-packed non-fiction is hard to beat. The **Dover Bookshop** (18 Earlham Street) has a good selection of the company's colouring, stencil and sticker books on subjects from Second World War aeroplanes to Victorian fashions. **Banana Bookshop** (10 The Market) is a bargain basement painted with trees and animals with a limited stock of reduced-price books, cards and toys. **Books etc** (26 James Street) has a small but well-chosen children's section.

Covent Garden is a good place for children's clothes shopping. The industrial-look **Dr Martens Dept Store** (1 King Street) has a children's section on level 4 that stocks brightly coloured boots from around £30, with toys and Playstations to entertain you while you wait. **Gap Kids** (121 Long Acre) specialises in serviceable denim and khaki, though it also runs a deluxe range that includes silk dresses and leather jackets. (Next door is a branch of Claire's Accessories, see page 10.20.) **Paul Smith** (40–44 Floral Street) is not as expensive as you might expect, and the clothes at least combine beautiful fabrics, unusual design and quality craftsmanship. **Monsoon** (5–6 James Street) has a rail of miniature hippie-style dresses with particularly attractive flower-strewn summer wear. It's also worth looking at the five stalls in The Market that sell designer children's

clothes including Sarah Brown and Ragamuffin. And if the little darlings want to buy something for you, send them to **Lush** (11 The Market), whose range of handmade cosmetics includes soaps and bubble baths with child-pleasing names (flying saucers, lush lime smoothie) and a selection of dusting powders they can scoop into boxes themselves.

The area is stacked with eateries. **TGI Friday** (6 Bedford Street) goes out of its way to make life fun for children and easy for parents (especially at weekend lunchtimes) with the help of balloons, colouring sheets, children's menus and often face-painting. *Moules* and *frites* restaurant **Belgo Centraal** (50 Earlham Street) is more welcoming to children than its severely trendy image would indicate – and you can't go far wrong with chips and ice cream. The self-service, semi-outdoor **Ponti's** in The Market has reasonably priced pasta, sandwiches and jacket potatoes and Neal's Yard has a couple of good vegetarian cafés and a bagel bar. **Häagen-Dazs**, also in The Market, has a restaurant and take-away service. Or if you've seriously overspent, grab a jacket potato from the stall in the Piazza and sit on the pavement to watch the free entertainment. vw

GETTING THERE Covent Garden Underground

Daisy & Tom

This is the children's 'department store' set up in 1997 by Tim Waterstone of bookshop fame. The interior is a fanciful mix of tented ceiling, candy-shop displays and murals depicting two children – Daisy and Tom, one assumes – in idyllic surroundings. There is a big wooden car to 'drive' and a ride-on merry-go-round that swings into action at 11.00, 13.00, 15.00 and 17.00 Monday to Saturday (Sunday, 13.00, 15.00 and 17.00).

You may feel that it's all just a touch too twee, but beneath the whimsy the shop works hard. The wide, wood-floored aisles and ramps of the downstairs toy department are perfect for buggies and rampaging children, and there is a wide selection of good-quality toys for tinies to 8-year-olds, including Playmobil, Lego, Plan Toys and the Daisy & Tom own range. (Daisy & Tom's key audience is the 0–8 age group, though the store's buyers allow for the fact that some 8-year-olds need bigger clothes/more challenging books and so on.) Price-wise, it all ranges from the extravagant – this is sw3 – to pocket-money level, so there are affordable treats to be had.

The book 'room' is quite a feature: around the centrepiece clock tower runs a balcony featuring carved wooden owls, cats and bears. It has an excellent selection of books for young ones, beginner readers, 5–8s and 8+ age groups, and at 11.30 and 16.30 each day (16.30 only on Sundays) hosts a storytime session.

The hair salon, next to the toy department, is one of those places where you can, if you must, get a certificate (including a photograph and lock of hair) to mark the occasion of your child's first haircut.

The self-service Soda Bar caters for sophisticated tastes, what with 'baby cappuccino' (frothy milk with chocolate sprinkles), Konditor and Cook cakes, made-to-order sandwiches and salads, and 100 per cent

natural baby foods (which can be warmed up for you, as can bottles of milk), plus wines and beers for the adults.

Upstairs in the shoe/clothes department you can watch a short, sweet marionette show of 'Peter and the Wolf' which runs every half hour, or buy fashions from the likes of Osh Kosh, French Connection, Elle, Baby Dior and – the latest word in children's fashion we're told – Dogwood and Maharishi. D&T's own basics range is good quality and not too expensive. Prices get a bit silly for the visions in velvet and chiffon – but they are lovely. There are changing rooms, a toilet (and a disabled toilet), and a baby-changing room. JL

ADDRESS 181 Kings Road, London SW3 (020 7352 5000)
OPEN Monday, Tuesday, Friday, 9.00–18.00; Wednesday, Thursday 9.00–19.00; Saturday, 9.30–18.30; Sunday, 12.00–18.00 (longer opening hours in run up to Christmas)
GETTING THERE Sloane Square Underground

Fan Club

Pam Trigg set up Fan Club, London's only specialist children's fancy-dress outlet, when she was offered some 300 costumes created for friends by René Jeanne, a costume-maker for the Royal Opera and Ballet, whom Trigg had encountered in the course of her career as a film and TV stylist. She now employs two designers and costume-makers herself and together they have expanded the collection using their own experience of what children like to elaborate on traditional outfits – for instance creating glamorous witches and devilinas with swathes of red organza and long red fingernails rather than the usual sombre Hallowe'en fare.

The shop interior is like a fantasy castle, with stained-glass windows, gold- and silver-painted ceilings, chandeliers and walls of many colours. As well as clients from the moving-image industries and schools, Fan Club kits out some 60 over-2s a week for parties and special occasions. Girls still want mostly to be flower fairies or princesses – though Fan Club princess outfits come with interesting extra details such as an Anne Boleyn wimple headdress with a veil edged in jewels. And Pam uses her skill as a stylist to put together entire costumes complete with shoes, jewellery, headgear and props, picking and mixing in response to the child's imagination. Boys go for pirates and knights or accessories such as the lavishly plumed Roman helmets, with swords and shields. Categories include animals, circus, cabaret, contemporary (the Spice Girls), historical, literary, national costume, sci-fi and uniforms. Retail outfits start at £65, though you can pick up accessories from £5; telephone for hire prices. vw

ADDRESS The Old Dairy, 133 Kilburn Lane, London W10 (020 8932 1313)
OPEN Monday to Saturday, 10.00–18.00
GETTING THERE Queen's Park Underground; free parking on side streets

Kensington

I've always found Kensington's obvious wealth deeply offputting – avenue upon avenue of homogeneous stuccoed housing that doesn't even pretend, like the more expensive parts of north London, to be little different from the streets the rest of us live in. But surprisingly, Kensington High Street is far from exclusive, with a concentration of shops for children that makes it worth trying out for one-stop shopping.

At the top end of the range is **What Katy Did** (49 Kensington Church Street), opened in 1999 by Kate Molloy. Prices here can be off the scale – frocks with the Simonetta label, for instance, retail at up to £150 – but there are also beautiful and unusual dresses at £30–£40 and Lucy Locket fantasy costumes (c. £30–£45) that rival anything on *Come Dancing!* On a more prosaic note, **M&S** (99 KHS) and **BHS** (101 KHS) both have small selections of reasonably priced clothes. **H&M Hennes** (123b KHS) sells good-value baby clothes – as long as you don't mind every garment being emblazoned with a rabbit or a teddy – and practical wear for 1–6s including an impressive range of denim. **0–12 Benetton** (129 KHS) is good for brightly coloured jumpers, sweatshirts and leggings, and there's also a branch of **Gap Kids** (146 KHS, see pages 10.10, 10.24). **Claire's Accessories** (169 KHS) is my friend's daughter's favourite shop: a riot of pink and silver, feathers, sequins, beads and hearts. £3.50 gets you the crown jewels – a silver tiara encrusted with blue and pink gems – while £2.50 provides a week's worth of rings and matching stick-on earrings.

Trotters (127 KHS) is a one-stop shop in its own right. At the back is a child-friendly Start-rite shoe shop; at the front are clothes from such labels as Paul Smith, Kenzo and Chipie. There are also soft toys, puzzles, a small but well-chosen case of books (excepting the complete set of Mr Men) and a hairdressing area with a spacecraft structure and flashing lights for entertainment.

Kensington

Argos (160–166 KHS) is unbeatable value for toys and particularly useful for large purchases (bicycles, slides, swings) that local shops don't have room for. There's also the advantage that you choose from a catalogue so there's very little on display and you don't suffer endless demands for goodies your children spot on the way to the till. Most of the Argos range falls in the 'I'm fantastic – I'm plastic' category; if you want something more hand-crafted try the **Hill Toy Co** (71 Abingdon Road).

Waterstone's (193 KHS) has a child-friendly area where you can spend as long as you wish pulling out books and a good, well-ordered reference section, though I was slightly dismayed to find the only non-Christian book on the religion shelves was *Sam's Passover*. **The Children's Book Centre** (237 KHS) is one of London's best children's bookshops, with more than 20,000 titles (see page 10.6). It also stocks toys – there's nothing exclusive here, but the range is such (Action Man, Barbie, board games, Brio, crafts kits, dressing-up clothes, Fisher Price, jigsaws, Lego, soft toys, Thomas) that you'd be almost guaranteed to find a present for a child of any age. And if it's you who's giving the party, **The Non-Stop Party Shop** (214–216 KHS) has a full range of disposable tableware, hats, poppers, etc, as well as bouncy castles, ball ponds and tables and chairs for hire.

Holland Park, at the west end of the High Street, has a pleasant café. There's a small sandy playground beside the Ilchester Place entrance near KHS or a big adventure playground and 1 o'clock club off Abbotsbury Road. If you're on your own and deserve a treat, try Leighton House (12 Holland Park Road) – the gallery bed projecting into the Arab Hall with its tinkling fountain fulfils my every fantasy. VW

GETTING THERE Kensington High Street Underground

Oxford Circus/Regent Street

You may feel, as many sane people do, that going anywhere near London's most furred-up artery, Oxford Circus, is a generally bad idea and that to do so with children is doubly mad. But there are compensations. One of them is **Borders** (203 Oxford Street) which as well as an excellent children's department hosting regular storytelling events (see page 10.2) has loos, baby-changing facilities and a café.

Most famously, of course, there's **Hamley's** (188 Regent Street) which bills itself as the 'finest toyshop in the world' and, while never quite living up to grown-up memories of what it used to be like, is toy heaven for most children. There are seven floors of teddies, dolls, cars, trains, kites, puzzles, games, books, dressing-up clothes, you name it, plus a café in the basement. Visit at Christmas and you'll find the population of a small country crammed inside.

Slaves to merchandising that we are, we rather like the **Warner Bros Studio Store**, just down the road at 172 Regent Street. Full of visual jokes (Sylvester creeping up Nelson's column to catch Tweety Pie, Superman in his telephone booth), it has the cast of Warners' characters emblazoned on everything from golf clubs to babygros – there are Bugs mugs, Taz tees, Batman cushions, Spiderman sweatshirts … More movie-related merchandising at **The Disney Store** (140 Regent Street) where the staff are cheery to the point of being irritating. (Your payment slip asks for the 'guest's signature' – none of that 'customer' nonsense here. Have a nice day.) Children usually love it. Where else, after all, can you get a glittery Little Mermaid rucksack or a furry speaking Winnie the Pooh notebook? There are steps down to the lower floor and no lift, but staff will, of course, help with buggies.

Down at **Gap Kids**, on the other hand (146 Regent Street, plus branches in Oxford Street), you can find the things you'd like them to like – sensible

and stylish sweatshirts, jeans and dresses. Just over the road is **Lego Kidswear** (37 Regent Street) while at number 198 is **Gymboree** – the only central London branch of this American retailer – selling a good selection of practical, reasonably priced children's clothes. Fashion victims should also check out **NikeTown** where – even if you don't want to indulge in an infant-sized pair of the hottest trainers – you can enjoy the entertaining spectacle of Oxford Circus' whizziest retail 'experience'.

A rather more traditional approach to retailing can be found in Oxford Street, at **John Lewis**, sister store of Peter Jones in Sloane Square. As well as being the place half middle-class London seemingly flocks on a Saturday to buy fridges/beds/vacuum cleaners/curtains, it also has a good range of children's clothes (especially shoes), a comprehensive baby department, helpful staff, a delivery service, café and mother-and-baby room. Not so much a shop, more a well-loved institution.

Just north of Oxford Street, the **BBC Shop** is also worth a mention. Part of the BBC Experience (see page 4.2) it sells a variety of Beeb-related merchandising, from model Daleks and books-of-the-series to Bob the Builder magazines and Camberwick Green videos.

The area isn't short of McDonald's and Burger Kings if you need somewhere to eat in a hurry. Alternatively there's a **PizzaExpress** in Langham Place. We lament the day that **R K Stanley** (6 Little Portland Street), home of a very superior sausage and mash, stopped doing Saturday lunches with free kids' meals – it used to make it all worthwhile. Perhaps they will have seen the light by the time this guide is published. See also **Yo! Sushi**, page 9.10. JL

GETTING THERE Oxford Circus Underground

The Party Superstore

There is something refreshingly old fashioned about the Party Superstore on Lavender Hill. In this shop, completely untouched by modern retail design, you'll find a vast selection of party items including jars of balloons, streamers, ribbons, and stacks of paper cups and napkins adorned with everything from ballerinas to Batman. There's a good selection of fancy-dress costumes too, ranging from Robin Hood, Zorro, a caveman and Elvis (would you really do that to your child?) to Snow White, Mulan, a mermaid and assorted fairies, plus lots of spangly wands, wings and tiaras, pirate hats, policemen's helmets, masks and false moustaches. (Downstairs is devoted to adult fancy dress of the saucy waitress/army officer/giant furry orange variety, all of which makes me wonder what other people get up to in their spare time and whether I get out enough …)

The Party Superstore stocks a variety of silly plastic novelty toys suitable for party bags or small treats, and – since this is also a joke shop – glass cases full of all those things children like but parents would prefer them not to: whoopee cushions, 'pet puke', 'horror finger', itching powder and worse (beware the 'adult' novelty items which take some explaining). It comes as no surprise that, according to an article from *The Times* which has been stuck on the wall, this is a favourite shop of comedian Harry Hill.

The Party Superstore also stocks ballet, tap and jazz shoes, tights and leotards. Hard to imagine what all those budding Darcy Bussells make of the place. JL

ADDRESS 268 Lavender Hill, London SW11 (020 7924 3210)
OPEN Monday to Wednesday, Friday and Saturday 9.00–18.00;
Thursday, 9.00–19.00; Sunday, 10.30–16.30
GETTING THERE Clapham Junction rail

Safeway, Camden

Oh, envy the happy people of Camden! For they have a Safeway super-store which has not only a dry-cleaners, a pharmacy and toilets (how handy), a coffee shop (how civilised – they will even warm baby bottles for you) and all the usual aisles of groceries, but also a crèche.

On presentation of the parent/carer's Safeway ABC card, children aged 2–8 can be left in the crèche for up to two and a half hours for about the cost of a couple of boxes of cornflakes: £1.25 per child for the first half hour; £2.50 for one hour; and £1.25 for each subsequent half hour. So they have a good time hurling themselves into the ball pool or clambering across the climbing frame while you glide around the aisles. You're asked not to leave the store while your child is in the crèche, and will be paged if there's a problem. An electronic security tag is attached to your clothes and your child's. It may be necessary to queue during peak periods. It's possible to hold children's parties in the crèche Monday to Wednesday between 14.00 and 18.00.

Safeway has another crèche at its Queensbury store (Honeypot Lane, NW9). Meanwhile the O2 Centre (see page 9.10) has a Sainsbury's and, on level 2, a 'Stay 'n' Play' crèche.

So there – grocery shopping and foul tempers don't have to go together. All supermarkets should be like this. (Honourable mention goes as well to the playroom at furniture superstore Ikea in Brent Park, NW10.) JL

ADDRESS Chalk Farm Road, London NW1 (020 7428 0405)
OPEN Monday to Saturday, 9.30–18.30; Sunday, 10.00–16.00 (last admission half an hour before closing)
GETTING THERE Chalk Farm Underground; ample free parking

index

kids london

Index

Index

Index

PICTURES
All pictures are by Keith Collie except: